for Extraordinary Ministers of Holy Communion

Living Liturgy™

for Extraordinary Ministers of Holy Communion

Year C • 2013

Joyce Ann Zimmerman, C.PP.S.
Kathleen Harmon, S.N.D. de N.
Christopher W. Conlon, S.M.

LITURGICAL PRESS
Collegeville, Minnesota

www.litpress.org

Design by Ann Blattner. Art by Julie Lonneman.

ISSN 1933-3129

ISBN 978-0-8146-3391-5

Presented to

_____

*in grateful appreciation
for ministering as an
Extraordinary Minister
of
Holy Communion*

_____

_____

(date)

USING THIS RESOURCE

By baptism we are all made members of the Body of Christ. Extraordinary ministers of Holy Communion are called to serve the Christian community by ministering the Body and Blood of Christ to the Body of Christ. Rather than a "status symbol" in the liturgical community, these ministers are servants of the servants, as Jesus himself showed us at the Last Supper. They are called "extraordinary" not because of any personal worthiness or honor but because the "ordinary" ministers of Holy Communion are bishops, priests, deacons, or instituted acolytes. In the typical parish situation, however, large numbers of the faithful come forward for Communion, and so in most cases lay members of the parish are designated as "extraordinary" ministers so that this part of the Mass does not become disproportionately long.

Preparing for this ministry

As with all ministry, extraordinary ministers of Holy Communion must prepare themselves for their ministry. This book is intended to be a guide and resource for that preparation. Each Sunday and some key feast days are laid out with the gospel text (or a shortened version of it), prayer, and reflections to help the Communion minister prepare each week, even when he or she is not scheduled for ministry. Some of the language of the text implies a group is present for the preparation; these texts are conveniently worded for when two or more extraordinary ministers gather for preparation, or for when these texts are shared in the context of the rite of Holy Communion with the homebound and sick.

Holy Communion for the homebound and sick

Jesus' preaching of the Good News in the gospel is made visible by his many and varied good works on behalf of others. Perhaps more than any other group, Jesus reaches out with his healing touch to those who are sick, and this compassionate ministry continues today in the life of the church. One of the many blessings of parishes that have extraordinary ministers of Holy Communion is that parishioners who are sick or homebound or those in hospitals and other care centers can share in the liturgical life of parishes more frequently. These ministers are reminded that the sick and suffering share in a special way in Jesus' passion. The ministers can bring hope and consolation and the strength of the Bread of Life to those who seem cut off from active participation in parish life.

Adapting this resource for Holy Communion for the homebound and sick

It is presumed that each Communion minister is familiar with the rites for Communion with the sick. There is a brief rite for those in hospitals or other care centers; this shorter rite is used when the circumstances would not permit the longer rite. The longer rite is used in ordinary circumstances and includes a Liturgy of the Word preceding the Communion rite. When using the longer rite, the opening and closing prayer of this book would nicely round out the beginning and end of the service; the gospel is conveniently included to proclaim the Word, and a reflection (also included in this book) may be shared.

Privilege and dignity

It is indeed a unique blessing to serve members of the parish as extraordinary ministers of Holy Communion, both at the parish Mass and by taking Communion to the sick and homebound. The parish's presence through ministry to the sick and homebound is a particular sign of their dignity as members of the Body of Christ. The Communion minister is in a unique position to offer hope and comfort to those who may find little in life to comfort them. May this ministry always be a sign of Jesus' great love and compassion for all his Father's beloved children!

As we begin this season of Advent, Christ is present with us now even as we await his final coming in glory. Let us prepare ourselves to celebrate this mystery of his presence to us now and always . . .

Prayer

O God who comes to us, we welcome you into our presence and open ourselves attentively to you. Be with us during this Advent as we prepare our hearts to receive you with fervor and devotion. We ask this through Christ our Lord. **Amen**.

Gospel (Luke 21:25-28, 34-36)

Jesus said to his disciples: "There will be signs in the sun, the moon, and the stars, and on earth nations will be in dismay, perplexed by the roaring of the sea and the waves. People will die of fright in anticipation of what is coming upon the world, for the powers of the heavens will be shaken. And then they will see the Son of Man coming in a cloud with power and great glory. But when these signs begin to happen, stand erect and raise your heads because your redemption is at hand.

"Beware that your hearts do not become drowsy from carousing and drunkenness and the anxieties of daily life, and that day catch you by surprise like a trap. For that day will assault everyone who lives on the face of the earth. Be vigilant at all times and pray that you have the strength to escape the tribulations that are imminent and to stand before the Son of Man."

Brief Silence

For Reflection

The gospel admonishes us to be vigilant for a future event—the Second Coming of "the Son of Man"—of which none of us has any experience. But this gospel is not really about the end of the world; it is about the completion of the kingdom. The Second Coming is not a deadline; it is an invitation and incentive to live in a certain way in the present time. The gospel calls us to be vigilant not about a future event but about a present way of living shaped by the Jesus before whom we stand. The signs of the end of the world are not disastrous cosmic events which we anticipate with dread, but the fullness of our own Gospel living.

The signs we ordinarily think will accompany the end of the world—cosmos in disarray and nations in dismay—are really signs of how far we still have to go to implant Gospel values in our lives and world. Our care and love for others, our fruitful response to the challenge of Gospel living, are the definitive signs of Christ's presence among us. These are the signs of God's kingdom coming to completion.

✦ In the faces of those to whom I distribute Holy Communion, I see "great glory" and this invites me to . . .

Brief Silence

Prayer

God of light and darkness, you come to us in the Holy Communion of your divine Son. Strengthen us and encourage us always to encounter you in the ordinary circumstances of our lives, live the Gospel your Son came to teach us, and be ourselves signs of your kingdom come. We ask this through Christ our Lord. **Amen**.

God kept Mary free from sin from the very moment of her conception in her mother's womb. As we begin our prayer, let us ask God to free us from our sinfulness and imitate more perfectly Mary's goodness . . .

Prayer

God of salvation, you sent your angel Gabriel to greet Mary as one "full of grace." Help us to model our lives after Mary's fidelity, always opening ourselves to the grace you offer us. We ask this through Christ our Lord. **Amen**

Gospel (Luke 1:26-38)

The angel Gabriel was sent from God to a town of Galilee called Nazareth, to a virgin betrothed to a man named Joseph, of the house of David, and the virgin's name was Mary. And coming to her, he said, "Hail, full of grace! The Lord is with you." But she was greatly troubled at what was said and pondered what sort of greeting this might be. Then the angel said to her, "Do not be afraid, Mary, for you have found favor with God. Behold, you will conceive in your womb and bear a son, and you shall name him Jesus. He will be great and will be called Son of the Most High, and the Lord God will give him the throne of David his father, and he will rule over the house of Jacob forever, and of his Kingdom there will be no end." But Mary said to the angel, "How can this be, since I have no relations with a man?" And the angel said to her in reply, "The Holy Spirit will come upon you, and the power of the Most High will overshadow you. Therefore the child to be born will be called holy, the Son of God. And behold, Elizabeth, your relative, has also conceived a son in her old age, and this is the sixth month for her who was called barren; for nothing will be

impossible for God." Mary said, "Behold, I am the handmaid of
the Lord. May it be done to me according to your word." Then the
angel departed from her.

Brief Silence

For Reflection

The Holy Spirit overshadowed Mary and she gave birth to the
"Son of the Most High." This was brought about in the aftermath
of Mary's pondering, questioning, and, finally, saying yes. Mary's
dialogue with Gabriel does not reveal obstinacy or belligerence or
unwillingness. The dialogue simply reveals that Mary truly did
have a choice. It reveals that Mary, while not knowing fully what
her yes would entail, was aware that she was encountering something totally out of the ordinary, she was encountering previously
unrevealed mystery.

We, too, are overshadowed by the Holy Spirit who enables us to
be holy and unblemished, adopted, beloved, chosen. Like Mary, we
ponder, question, and, finally, say yes by how we live. Like Mary,
our dialogues with God, self, others that bring us to say yes are
not weakness or hesitation. Like Mary, we must respond to God's
offer of grace with our "Behold, I am the handmaid [servant] of
the Lord." Then, like Mary, we, too, bear the Son of God within us.
She is the model for God-bearing. She is our Mother and helps us
attain for ourselves the fruits of her great privilege—bearing in
her being Emmanuel, God is with us!

✦ Where I am resistant to saying "May it be done unto me according to your word" is . . . What helps me say yes is . . .

Brief Silence

Prayer

God of holiness and life, you call all of us to share in the salvation
you offer. Help us to ponder, question, but always say yes with full
hearts to whatever you ask of us. We ask this through Christ our
Lord. **Amen**.

John the Baptist calls us to "[p]repare the way of the Lord." As we prepare to pray well, let us consider how we have not stayed on a straight path to the Lord in our daily living . . .

Prayer

Merciful God, you have always sent prophets among us to call us to be faithful to you. Guide us along straight paths and help us to be faithful in doing your will. We ask this through Christ our Lord. **Amen**.

Gospel (Luke 3:1-6)

In the fifteenth year of the reign of Tiberius Caesar, when Pontius Pilate was governor of Judea, and Herod was tetrarch of Galilee, and his brother Philip tetrarch of the region of Ituraea and Trachonitis, and Lysanias was tetrarch of Abilene, during the high priesthood of Annas and Caiaphas, the word of God came to John the son of Zechariah in the desert. John went throughout the whole region of the Jordan, proclaiming a baptism of repentance for the forgiveness of sins, as it is written in the book of the words of the prophet Isaiah: / *A voice of one crying out in the desert: / "Prepare the way of the Lord, / make straight his paths. / Every valley shall be filled / and every mountain and hill shall be made low. / The winding roads shall be made straight, / and the rough ways made smooth, / and all flesh shall see the salvation of God."*

Brief Silence

For Reflection

John proclaims that we must "[p]repare the way of the Lord" by repenting. He describes repentance as a leveling and a straightening out of the uneven and crooked shape of our lives. When the paths of our lives are not straight and smooth, we cannot be free to enter wholeheartedly into our journey toward God. If our eyes are too closely focused on the rocks and crags of our lives, we cannot see the presence of God beckoning us toward smoother going. John's image of a straight and smooth way is a metaphoric, descriptive definition of repentance. It is his (and Advent's) way to call us to faithful living in right relationship with God.

John calls us to ask whether our path is taking us closer to God as well as opening up for others the way to God. Smooth paths are those which help us focus on God and root out anything that keeps us from God. Smooth paths are those which increase our love for God and others, prompting us to bring others along the same smooth and straight path on which we are journeying toward final fulfillment with God. Then "all flesh shall see the salvation of God."

✦ Like the Eucharist, I am food for others as they struggle to straighten and make smooth the paths of their lives in that . . .

Brief Silence

Prayer

O God who guides and protects, you are with us on our journey of life. Help us to keep ourselves focused on you and never lose sight of your love and presence. We ask this through Christ our Lord. **Amen**.

We gather to hear and ponder the good news of Christ's coming. Let us quiet our hearts so that we may encounter this Good News in our prayer and sharing . . .

Prayer

God of Good News, you sent John to announce the coming of your Son, the Messiah. Be with us as we prepare to open our hearts to Jesus' many comings, help us hear his word of salvation to us, and encourage us to respond with generous care for others. We ask this through Christ our Lord. **Amen**.

Gospel (Luke 3:10-18)

The crowds asked John the Baptist, "What should we do?" He said to them in reply, "Whoever has two cloaks should share with the person who has none. And whoever has food should do likewise." Even tax collectors came to be baptized and they said to him, "Teacher, what should we do?" He answered them, "Stop collecting more than what is prescribed." Soldiers also asked him, "And what is it that we should do?" He told them, "Do not practice extortion, do not falsely accuse anyone, and be satisfied with your wages."

Now the people were filled with expectation, and all were asking in their hearts whether John might be the Christ. John answered them all, saying, "I am baptizing you with water, but one mightier than I is coming. I am not worthy to loosen the thongs of his sandals. He will baptize you with the Holy Spirit and fire. His winnowing fan is in his hand to clear his threshing floor and to gather the wheat into his barn, but the chaff he will burn with unquenchable fire." Exhorting them in many other ways, he preached good news to the people.

Brief Silence

For Reflection

John's clear and unequivocal answers to "What should we do?" gave direction to people's lives. He challenged the crowds and tax collectors and soldiers to change their behavior, to make other people their focus and care. John's good news, however, went beyond merely telling the people how to behave toward each other, but also instilled expectation in them. His answers indicated that something new is happening. His good news pointed to the One who is all Good News, a mighty Savior who is in our midst, who is near. The Good News is not a message but a person—Jesus.

"What should we do?" The gospel gives a simple challenge: make Jesus the center of our lives. Make how he responded to people the way we respond to people. Make his fire well up in our hearts so that our baptism with the Holy Spirit conforms us more perfectly to him. Make our answer to the question one that leads us to preach to others the same Good News Jesus preached to us. And we must preach the same way he did: not simply with words, but with deeds.

✦ I see Jesus, the Good News, in those who come to me for Holy Communion whenever I . . . They help me to know what I should do in that . . .

Brief Silence

Prayer

Loving God, you guide us in right ways. Be with us as we discover anew what it is you ask of us. Help us to be faithful to our baptismal promises, loving and serving you in all things. We ask this through Christ our Lord. **Amen**.

Elizabeth recognized the infant in Mary's womb as her Lord. Let us reflect on how we recognize the Lord in our lives and prepare for his coming . . .

Prayer

O God, you sent your Spirit to be with Elizabeth so she would recognize the Lord coming to her. Send your Spirit upon us so that we might recognize the presence of your divine Son in all we meet and experience. We ask this through Christ our Lord. **Amen**.

Gospel (Luke 1:39-45)

Mary set out and traveled to the hill country in haste to a town of Judah, where she entered the house of Zechariah and greeted Elizabeth. When Elizabeth heard Mary's greeting, the infant leaped in her womb, and Elizabeth, filled with the Holy Spirit, cried out in a loud voice and said, "Blessed are you among women, and blessed is the fruit of your womb. And how does this happen to me, that the mother of my Lord should come to me? For at the moment the sound of your greeting reached my ears, the infant in my womb leaped for joy. Blessed are you who believed that what was spoken to you by the Lord would be fulfilled."

Brief Silence

For Reflection

Mary went in haste to Elizabeth's house, entered, and greeted her. Elizabeth recognized and responded to the mystery taking place. She expressed astonishment, wonder, amazement: "how does this happen to me, that the mother of my Lord should come to me?" There is encounter. There is blessing. There is praise. One woman carries the infant who is born to be precursor. The other carries the infant who is born to be Savior.

It is too easy to dismiss this encounter. We might be astonished at the singularity of these two women; we might wonder at their holiness and obedience; we might be amazed at their openness to God's grace. An even greater astonishment, wonder, amazement, however, is also at work: the Lord himself comes to *us*. How do *we* respond? Mary responded by believing and saying yes to God's will. Elizabeth responded by opening herself to be a participant in the mystery of salvation and uttering praise and blessing when she encountered her Lord. Our response to the mystery of the Word made flesh must be similar to theirs: believing, saying yes, praising, blessing. This response primes us to celebrate the mystery of Christmas in all its fullness.

✦ Beyond bringing Holy Communion to the sick and homebound, I myself am a presence of Christ for others when I . . .

Brief Silence

Prayer

O God, you fill us with wonder and amazement with your constant presence to us. Strengthen our belief in you, that we might always bring your presence to others through our love and good works. We ask this through Christ our Lord. **Amen**.

During this holy season, we lift our hearts with joy to praise our God who sends his Son to dwell among us. Let us prepare ourselves to hear the word of salvation and receive the gift of life God offers us . . .

Prayer

God of glory, we come to you in praise as the shepherds sang long ago. May we be filled with your glory and bring joy to all we meet during this holy season. We ask this through Christ our Lord. **Amen**.

Gospel (Luke 2:1-14; at the Mass during the Night)

In those days a decree went out from Caesar Augustus that the whole world should be enrolled. This was the first enrollment, when Quirinius was governor of Syria. So all went to be enrolled, each to his own town. And Joseph too went up from Galilee from the town of Nazareth to Judea, to the city of David that is called Bethlehem, because he was of the house and family of David, to be enrolled with Mary, his betrothed, who was with child. While they were there, the time came for her to have her child, and she gave birth to her firstborn son. She wrapped him in swaddling clothes and laid him in a manger, because there was no room for them in the inn.

Now there were shepherds in that region living in the fields and keeping the night watch over their flock. The angel of the Lord appeared to them and the glory of the Lord shone around them, and they were struck with great fear. The angel said to them, "Do not be afraid; for behold, I proclaim to you good news of great joy that will be for all the people. For today in the city of David a savior has been born for you who is Christ and Lord. And this will be a sign for you: you will find an infant wrapped in swaddling clothes and lying in a manger." And suddenly there was a multitude of the heavenly host with the angel, praising God and saying: / "Glory to God in the highest / and on earth peace to those on whom his favor rests."

Brief Silence

For Reflection

The Savior of the world was born during the night of the year when darkness is the longest. Jesus comes for the people in dark places. The real, lasting, and deep joy of Christmas is that the Light shines wherever this King-Savior is acknowledged and adored. Now we are the shepherds surrounded by God's glory, whose very lives must sing "Glory to God in the highest." Now we are to find our home in this King-Savior.

In a manger, in a town far away, among shepherds, and in the dark of night, Jesus was born. Our salvation dawned in the messiness, poverty, and weakness of ordinary human life. This hardly seems like a very auspicious beginning to the dawn of salvation! Yet, we have hope not because we are perfect or because our world is perfect, but because Jesus was born into the house and family of our humanity. His birth gives us a new home and calls us to come home. His birth dispels darkness and raises us up to new heights with the Light of life. This is what this birth brought about: we dispel darkness and bring light by how we live. We come home.

✦ Like the angels and shepherds that first Christmas night, I glorify and praise God by . . .

Brief Silence

Prayer

O God, you bring strength out of weakness and light out of darkness. Be with us as we celebrate the joy of the birth of your divine Son, help us to be his light for others, and bring us home to you in everlasting life. We ask this through Christ our Lord. **Amen**.

We are God's family seeking to be in our Father's house. Let us open our hearts to the gift of God's grace and mercy . . .

Prayer

Father in heaven, just as your divine Son sought to be in your house, so do we seek your presence. Be with us during our prayer, that we might hear your voice and grow in wisdom and favor. We ask this through Christ our Lord. **Amen**.

Gospel **(Luke 2:41-52)**

Each year Jesus' parents went to Jerusalem for the feast of Passover, and when he was twelve years old, they went up according to festival custom. After they had completed its days, as they were returning, the boy Jesus remained behind in Jerusalem, but his parents did not know it. Thinking that he was in the caravan, they journeyed for a day and looked for him among their relatives and acquaintances, but not finding him, they returned to Jerusalem to look for him. After three days they found him in the temple, sitting in the midst of the teachers, listening to them and asking them questions, and all who heard him were astounded at his understanding and his answers. When his parents saw him, they were astonished, and his mother said to him, "Son, why have you done this to us? Your father and I have been looking for you with great anxiety." And he said to them, "Why were you looking for me? Did you not know that I must be in my Father's house?" But they did not understand what he said to them. He went down with them and came to Nazareth, and was obedient to them; and his mother kept all these things in her heart. And Jesus advanced in wisdom and age and favor before God and man.

Brief Silence

For Reflection

In this gospel, Mary and Joseph lost Jesus. They searched for him according to a predictable pattern: first, among their relatives, then they retraced their steps looking for him wherever they had been. Following this pattern led to finding Jesus. But their search also reveals another pattern, one significant for us and our daily living.

We look for Jesus when we, like him, seek to be in God's presence; when we, like him, choose to be obedient; when we, like him, grow in wisdom. Along the way we discover that Jesus enlarges where we look for him, how we find him, and what new understanding comes to us through our encounters with him. This is the pattern of faithful Christian living that brings us to fullness of life. Looking for Jesus is probably not a conscious element of our daily living, at least not in the sense that Mary and Joseph looked for him as told in the gospel. Yet, every time we seek to be in God's presence, choose to be obedient to what God wants of us, go out of our way to love one another, we are seeking Jesus. And we will always find him.

✦ I look for Jesus . . . I find him . . .

Brief Silence

Prayer

God of the Temple and God who is present to us, you call us always to your divine presence. Strengthen us by our communion with each other so that we might seek you with sincere hearts. We ask this through Christ our Lord. **Amen**.

Mary was blessed in becoming the mother of the divine Son. At the beginning of this New Year, we pause to reflect on God's blessings to us in Christ . . .

Prayer

Life-giving God, as we celebrate the motherhood of Mary, you shower us with life and holiness. Bless us as we strive to bring the life of your Son's Gospel to all we meet during this new year. We ask this through Christ our Lord. **Amen**.

Gospel (Luke 2:16-21)

The shepherds went in haste to Bethlehem and found Mary and Joseph, and the infant lying in the manger. When they saw this, they made known the message that had been told them about this child. All who heard it were amazed by what had been told them by the shepherds. And Mary kept all these things, reflecting on them in her heart. Then the shepherds returned, glorifying and praising God for all they had heard and seen, just as it had been told to them.

When eight days were completed for his circumcision, he was named Jesus, the name given him by the angel before he was conceived in the womb.

Brief Silence

For Reflection

This solemnity's gospel begins with the shepherds making haste after the angels announced to them that a Savior was born in Bethlehem. No dilly-dallying around to secure the sheep or change into clean clothes or even check on the truth of what had been told them. The angels' announcement was so startling, interesting, exciting, extraordinary that they made haste.

Having heard the angels' announcement of the birth of the Savior, the shepherds "went in haste" to find him. But it doesn't seem like the shepherds dilly-dallied around, either, once they found "the infant lying in the manger." This encounter propelled them into further quick action. Having found him, they returned to their sheep, their everyday life, but they were no longer the same shepherds. Their encounter with the newborn Infant had changed them: they became messengers of the Good News of Jesus' birth and could not stop "glorifying and praising God for all they had seen and heard." While the search for Jesus is important—we must find him—our response to finding him is even more important. This is the pattern for response to the Christmas mystery: come to Jesus, find him, and be changed.

✦ What hastens me to seek Jesus is . . . This changes me when . . .

Brief Silence

Prayer

O glorious God, the shepherds went in haste to find the newborn Infant, and then hastened to spread the Good News of his birth. Help us to glorify you in all things, to be faithful in spreading the Good News of salvation revealed by your divine Son, and bring us to share in everlasting glory with you. We ask this through Christ our Lord. **Amen**.

The magi were guided by the light of God's star to the newborn King. Let us open ourselves to God's light guiding us to encounter God's mercy and love during our prayer and reflection . . .

Prayer

God of universal salvation, you guided the magi to your newborn Son and they offered him homage and gifts. Draw us to that same divine Son, and help us to love him deeply and offer him the gift of our very selves. We ask this through Christ our Lord. **Amen**.

Gospel (Matt 2:1-12)

When Jesus was born in Bethlehem of Judea, in the days of King Herod, behold, magi from the east arrived in Jerusalem, saying, "Where is the newborn king of the Jews? We saw his star at its rising and have come to do him homage." When King Herod heard this, he was greatly troubled, and all Jerusalem with him. Assembling all the chief priests and the scribes of the people, he inquired of them where the Christ was to be born. They said to him, "In Bethlehem of Judea, for thus it has been written through the prophet: / *And you, Bethlehem, land of Judah, / are by no means least among the rulers of Judah; / since from you shall come a ruler, / who is to shepherd my people Israel."* / Then Herod called the magi secretly and ascertained from them the time of the star's appearance. He sent them to Bethlehem and said, "Go and search diligently for the child. When you have found him, bring me word, that I too may go and do him homage." After their audience with the king they set out. And behold, the star that they had seen at its rising preceded them, until it came and stopped over the place where the child was. They were overjoyed at seeing the star, and on entering the house they saw the child with Mary his mother. They prostrated themselves and did him homage.

Then they opened their treasures and offered him gifts of gold, frankincense, and myrrh. And having been warned in a dream not to return to Herod, they departed for their country by another way.

Brief Silence

For Reflection

Arriving in Jerusalem, the magi ask, "Where is the newborn king of the Jews?" This is the burning question that prompted them to follow a distant star to a distant place. What planted this burning question in their hearts surely was some wisdom that their lives were not complete; no doubt they experienced a restlessness that prompted them to follow the light of a star. Their journey to find the Infant was long and convoluted, yet guided by heavenly light.

We, too, will find Christ if we search. We, too, will be led by God's light. We, too, will be satisfied with fullness of life. What leads us and prompts us to seek the divine is more than simple light; it is always God's power acting in Christ to lead us to encounter the divine. The Light brings us to God and elicits from us the homage we instinctually know we must render God. The magi's epiphany journey is the pattern of our Christian living: we follow God's promptings, seek God diligently, overcome many obstacles, and finally, finding God, we offer homage and give over the treasure of our heart. We offer God the greatest gift we can— our very selves.

✦ Like the magi, I feel a driving desire to find Christ when . . .

Brief Silence

Prayer

God of light, life, and hope, like the magi of long ago we seek you and find you when we open ourselves to your guidance. May we be faithful in offering you the treasure of our hearts, our very selves. In this may we always bring you honor and glory. We ask this through Christ our Lord. **Amen.**

John points to Jesus as One greater than himself who baptizes with the Holy Spirit. Let us open our hearts to this Spirit who dwells within us, that we may be pleasing to God in all we do . . .

Prayer

O God of love, you shower your pleasure upon us, your beloved children, who have been baptized with water and the Holy Spirit. Help us to be faithful to our identity as your beloved ones, and to live the Gospel as Jesus taught us. We ask this through Christ our Lord. **Amen**.

Gospel (Luke 3:15-16, 21-22)

The people were filled with expectation, and all were asking in their hearts whether John might be the Christ. John answered them all, saying, "I am baptizing you with water, but one mightier than I is coming. I am not worthy to loosen the thongs of his sandals. He will baptize you with the Holy Spirit and fire."

After all the people had been baptized and Jesus also had been baptized and was praying, heaven was opened and the Holy Spirit descended upon him in bodily form like a dove. And a voice came from heaven, "You are my beloved Son; with you I am well pleased."

Brief Silence

For Reflection

Because of the power of John's baptism, the expectation of the people in the gospel is that they have found the Christ in John. John points the people, however, to Jesus who will bring an even more powerful baptism. This is the baptism each of us has received. This is the baptism that showers on us unexpected gifts. The Holy Spirit descended on Jesus, so does the Holy Spirit descend upon us; Jesus is the beloved Son, so are we beloved children; God was well pleased with Jesus, so is God well pleased with us.

All of us who share in the wisdom of Christian living through the years know that it takes a whole lifetime to repent, to turn toward God, to internalize the appropriate response to the great gifts God freely and lovingly gives us. Baptismal living takes a lifetime of fidelity. It takes a lifetime of learning. It takes a lifetime of discerning expectations—our own and God's—and doing whatever we need to fulfill those expectations. It takes a lifetime of opening ourselves to the Holy Spirit, hearing God's voice calling us beloved, living in such a way that God continues to be well pleased in us.

✦ I relate my ministry to my baptismal living in these ways . . .

Brief Silence

Prayer

God of love, give us the patience to grow in wisdom and self-giving, so that we can be faithful to our baptismal commitment. May we grow in our relationship with you, learn to love you more deeply, and live our lives with the guidance of the Holy Spirit. We ask this through Christ our Lord. **Amen.**

This Sunday's gospel tells the story of the wedding feast at Cana where Jesus reveals his glory. As we stand before the glory of God, let us open ourselves to God's divine presence during our time of reflection and prayer . . .

Prayer

God of abundance, you provide us with all good things. Be with us as we strive to believe in you more fervently, care for others more diligently, and love others with your love. We ask this through Christ our Lord. **Amen**.

Gospel (John 2:1-11)

There was a wedding at Cana in Galilee, and the mother of Jesus was there. Jesus and his disciples were also invited to the wedding. When the wine ran short, the mother of Jesus said to him, "They have no wine." And Jesus said to her, "Woman, how does your concern affect me? My hour has not yet come." His mother said to the servers, "Do whatever he tells you." Now there were six stone water jars there for Jewish ceremonial washings, each holding twenty to thirty gallons. Jesus told them, "Fill the jars with water." So they filled them to the brim. Then he told them, "Draw some out now and take it to the headwaiter." So they took it. And when the headwaiter tasted the water that had become wine, without knowing where it came from—although the servers who had drawn the water knew—, the headwaiter called the bridegroom and said to him, "Everyone serves good wine first, and then when people have drunk freely, an inferior one; but you have kept the good wine until now." Jesus did this as the beginning of his signs at Cana in Galilee and so revealed his glory, and his disciples began to believe in him.

Brief Silence

For Reflection

Jesus' epiphany—the revelation of his glory—did not end with
the sign he performed but with the belief to which his followers
came. Not only does Jesus change water into wine, but he transforms his disciples from being mere companions to becoming
those who believe in him. They move from fellowship to the intimacy of belief and their lives will never be the same. He changed
them. He will change us. And our lives will never be the same.

The intimacy of belief is not passive. This is Jesus' true glory
and his whole ministry: not only turning water into wine but
spending himself for the good of others. His total attentiveness
and response to others is the model for our own active believing,
the way to sustain intimacy with him, and is the promise of our
own glory. This kind of active believing changes us into those
who do as Jesus did. Here is the Good News: spending oneself for
the sake of another is how we actively believe, how we achieve
salvation, how we march steadily toward messianic abundance,
how we share in Jesus' glory. No, our lives will never be the same.

✦ Distributing the Body (or Blood) of Christ changes me when
I . . .

Brief Silence

Prayer

God of glory, you invite us to share in your Son's Body and Blood
in Holy Communion, and thus we share in your divine glory.
Help us to do all we can to shine forth your glory to all those to
whom we minister, to all those we encounter each day. We ask this
through Christ our Lord. **Amen.**

Jesus inaugurates his public ministry in the power of the Spirit. Let us prepare ourselves to pray well as we hear his Good News and share his Presence and love . . .

Prayer

Gracious God, your Spirit anointed your divine Son to bring glad tidings to those who need a word of compassion and comfort. Be with us as we hear those same words, strengthen us to live the Good News, and help us to cooperate with that same Spirit in fulfilling your Son's saving mission. We ask this through Christ our Lord. **Amen**.

Gospel (Luke 1:1-4; 4:14-21)

Since many have undertaken to compile a narrative of the events that have been fulfilled among us, just as those who were eyewitnesses from the beginning and ministers of the word have handed them down to us, I too have decided, after investigating everything accurately anew, to write it down in an orderly sequence for you, most excellent Theophilus, so that you may realize the certainty of the teachings you have received.

Jesus returned to Galilee in the power of the Spirit, and news of him spread throughout the whole region. He taught in their synagogues and was praised by all.

He came to Nazareth, where he had grown up, and went according to his custom into the synagogue on the sabbath day. He stood up to read and was handed a scroll of the prophet Isaiah. He unrolled the scroll and found the passage where it was written: / *The Spirit of the Lord is upon me, / because he has anointed me / to bring glad tidings to the poor. / He has sent me to proclaim liberty to captives / and recovery of sight to the blind, / to let the oppressed go free, / and to proclaim a year acceptable to the Lord.* / Rolling up the scroll, he handed it back to the attendant and sat down, and the eyes of all in the synagogue looked intently at him. He said to them, "Today this Scripture passage is fulfilled in your hearing."

Brief Silence

For Reflection

Luke portrays Jesus as One who had a clear understanding of who he was and his mission. Who he was: the One "in the power of the Spirit." His mission: "to bring glad tidings" to the poor, captives, blind, oppressed. But the Good News cannot be proclaimed only by Jesus. Those who come after Jesus are "to bring glad tidings" in many ways to many people. Luke wrote a gospel, and in this fulfilled who he was and his mission. Now we ourselves are to be the bearers of the Good News so that others may "realize the certainty" of the story we have received. We are certain about our story and how we live when Jesus is the model from whom we draw our words and make the decisions which shape our life. We are certain when we speak "in the power of the Spirit." It is not our words we speak, but God's words of eternal life. The gospel each of us writes is written by the way we live. And when this living is in accordance with the Gospel, then we fulfill who we are and our mission, too.

♦ The manner of my distributing Holy Communion arouses in others the certainty of the Good News in that . . .

Brief Silence

Prayer

O God who speaks the word of eternal life, be with us as we hear your word, taste the goodness of your gift of heavenly Food, and faithfully continue Jesus' saving mission. We ask this through Christ our Lord. **Amen.**

In this Sunday's gospel Jesus is a prophet not accepted in his hometown. As we prepare to encounter Jesus during our prayer, we ask God to open our ears so that we may receive Jesus and his word wholeheartedly . . .

Prayer

O God, you speak a stirring word to us which both comforts and challenges. Help us to hear your words, to make them our own, and to live them with courage and steadfastness. We ask this through Christ our Lord. **Amen**.

Gospel (Luke 4:21-30)

Jesus began speaking in the synagogue, saying: "Today this Scripture passage is fulfilled in your hearing." And all spoke highly of him and were amazed at the gracious words that came from his mouth. They also asked, "Isn't this the son of Joseph?" He said to them, "Surely you will quote me this proverb, 'Physician, cure yourself,' and say, 'Do here in your native place the things that we heard were done in Capernaum.'" And he said, "Amen, I say to you, no prophet is accepted in his own native place. Indeed, I tell you, there were many widows in Israel in the days of Elijah when the sky was closed for three and a half years and a severe famine spread over the entire land. It was to none of these that Elijah was sent, but only to a widow in Zarephath in the land of Sidon. Again, there were many lepers in Israel during the time of Elisha the prophet; yet not one of them was cleansed, but only Naaman the Syrian." When the people in the synagogue heard this, they were all filled with fury. They rose up, drove him out of the town, and led him to the brow of the hill on which their town had been built, to hurl him down headlong. But Jesus passed through the midst of them and went away.

Brief Silence

For Reflection

We are hearing words from Jesus at the very beginning of his public ministry as reported by Luke. The first line of this Sunday's gospel is the last line from last Sunday's gospel: "Today this Scripture passage is fulfilled in your hearing." Jesus speaks "gracious words" to the people of Nazareth about bringing glad tidings of freedom for captives and the oppressed, sight for the blind (see last Sunday's gospel). These words, however, are not only applied to Jesus and his ministry, but to the people as well. Hearing these words challenges the people themselves to do what they hear (thus are the words "fulfilled in your hearing"), and for this they reject Jesus and want to destroy him.

Yet God, whose word Jesus speaks, delivers him ("passed through the midst of them"). Eventually enemies do destroy Jesus on the cross. But do they? In the end God's gracious words of deliverance prevail. The ultimate word is Jesus; the ultimate deliverance is risen life, which is ours when we hear and heed the gracious divine words spoken to us. When God's words satisfy us, we are faced with the goodness in ourselves and how we are already responding to God. When God's words make demands on us, we are faced with new ways we must die to ourselves in order to become better disciples.

♦ What sustains me to live Jesus' words even in face of opposition and anger from others is . . .

Brief Silence

Prayer

Gracious God, you speak to us gracious divine words which call us to be prophets to all those we meet. Be with us as we strive to be faithful to the word you speak to us, to allow that word to change us, and to draw comfort from your abiding presence when we meet opposition. We ask this through Christ our Lord. **Amen**.

Simon Peter, James, and John left everything to follow Jesus. Let us reflect on our response to Jesus' call and our willingness to be his disciples . . .

Prayer

O God, your call is sure, your presence is abiding, and your help is generous. Help us to hear your call, to follow your Son faithfully in all we do, and to journey steadfastly toward the fullness of life you offer us. We ask this through Christ our Lord. **Amen**.

Gospel (Luke 5:1-11)

While the crowd was pressing in on Jesus and listening to the word of God, he was standing by the Lake of Gennesaret. He saw two boats there alongside the lake; the fishermen had disembarked and were washing their nets. Getting into one of the boats, the one belonging to Simon, he asked him to put out a short distance from the shore. Then he sat down and taught the crowds from the boat. After he had finished speaking, he said to Simon, "Put out into deep water and lower your nets for a catch." Simon said in reply, "Master, we have worked hard all night and have caught nothing, but at your command I will lower the nets." When they had done this, they caught a great number of fish and their nets were tearing. They signaled to their partners in the other boat to come to help them. They came and filled both boats so that the boats were in danger of sinking. When Simon Peter saw this, he fell at the knees of Jesus and said, "Depart from me, Lord, for I am a sinful man." For astonishment at the catch of fish they had made seized him and all those with him, and likewise James and John, the sons of

Zebedee, who were partners of Simon. Jesus said to Simon, "Do not be afraid; from now on you will be catching men." When they brought their boats to the shore, they left everything and followed him.

Brief Silence

For Reflection

Simon Peter begins a more sure relationship with Jesus by allowing him to take command of his boat. He moves to allowing Jesus to take command of his heart, openly confessing the truth about himself ("I am a sinful man"). Finally, he allows Jesus to take command of his whole life ("left everything and followed him"). Like Peter, we are to allow Jesus to take command of us—our possessions, our hearts, our lives. We are to see that what is at stake in Jesus' commands to us is life-threatening and life-giving. Life-threatening because choosing to follow Jesus costs us our all—we "leave everything." At the same time, we receive all—more than even an abundant "catch of fish," we receive Life.

The gospel makes clear that while God is present to us and calls us, our freedom is respected—God truly does give us a choice about answering the call. Jesus merely announces to Peter, "from now on you will be catching men." Peter was free to respond or not. Such is divine graciousness—God calls, but in the divine encounter gives us the strength and grace to respond.

♦ The privilege of distributing Holy Communion calls me to . . . in my daily living.

Brief Silence

Prayer

Gracious God, our communion with you helps us to surrender to you our possessions, our hearts, our lives. Be with us as we overcome whatever keeps us from being faithful to your call and help us to open ourselves more fervently to the abundant life you offer us. We ask this through Christ our Lord. **Amen**.

With this day we begin Lent, a time focused on conversion and spiritual growth. Let us pray that we might respond with willing hearts to God's overtures of mercy and forgiveness.

Prayer

Merciful God, you forgive those who come to you asking for wholeness and peace. Be with us during our Lenten journey so that we might come to Easter with renewed hearts, whole hearts, giving hearts. We ask this through Christ our Lord. **Amen**.

Gospel (Matt 6:1-6, 16-18)

Jesus said to his disciples: "Take care not to perform righteous deeds in order that people may see them; otherwise, you will have no recompense from your heavenly Father. When you give alms, do not blow a trumpet before you, as the hypocrites do in the synagogues and in the streets to win the praise of others. Amen, I say to you, they have received their reward. But when you give alms, do not let your left hand know what your right is doing, so that your almsgiving may be secret. And your Father who sees in secret will repay you.

"When you pray, do not be like the hypocrites, who love to stand and pray in the synagogues and on street corners so that others may see them. Amen, I say to you, they have received their reward. But when you pray, go to your inner room, close the door, and pray to your Father in secret. And your Father who sees in secret will repay you.

"When you fast, do not look gloomy like the hypocrites. They neglect their appearance, so that they may appear to others to be fasting. Amen, I say to you, they have received their reward. But when you fast, anoint your head and wash your face, so that you may not appear to be fasting, except to your Father who is hidden. And your Father who sees what is hidden will repay you."

Brief Silence

For Reflection

Lenten penance is not about self-denial for its own sake, but is directed toward renewing our relationship with others, God, and self through acts of charity, prayer, and fasting. Lenten penance is not undertaken for our own sake (to receive rewards), but for the sake of returning to God with our whole heart. The gospel teaching about penance makes clear that renewed relationships can only be realized through the self-denial that turns us away from ourselves. We deny self so that we may better give self. A whole heart is a giving heart.

The task of renewing relationships necessitates a forgetfulness of self that compels self-giving. In the gospel Jesus points beyond *behaviors* to a *conversion* of heart. This kind of conversion demands of us a unique self-giving—a forgetting about ourselves which places God at the very center of our lives. Behaviors are important, to be sure; changed behaviors and habits are also a goal of Lent and often witness to a conversion of heart. But changed behaviors are worthless if they don't lead to and express something deeper: that conversion of heart which brings us closer to God and each other. A whole heart is a giving heart.

♦ I experience having a whole heart when . . . having a giving heart when . . .

Brief Silence

Prayer

Loving God, you never abandon us on our Lenten journey of conversion. Be with us during these weeks, help us to grow in our communion with you and each other, and bring us to fullness of life. We ask this through Christ our Lord. **Amen**.

As we pause for reflection and prayer during this first week of Lent, let us ask for forgiveness for the times we have given in to temptation . . .

Prayer

O God of power and might, your Son never swerved from who he was but always remained true to himself. Help us during this time of conversion and renewal to remain true to ourselves as your beloved sons and daughters, and to resist whatever temptations take us farther away from you. We ask this through Christ our Lord. **Amen**.

Gospel (Luke 4:1-13)

Filled with the Holy Spirit, Jesus returned from the Jordan and was led by the Spirit into the desert for forty days, to be tempted by the devil. He ate nothing during those days, and when they were over he was hungry. The devil said to him, "If you are the Son of God, command this stone to become bread." Jesus answered him, "It is written, *One does not live on bread alone*." Then he took him up and showed him all the kingdoms of the world in a single instant. The devil said to him, "I shall give to you all this power and glory; for it has been handed over to me, and I may give it to whomever I wish. All this will be yours, if you worship me." Jesus said to him in reply, "It is written: / *You shall worship the Lord, your God, / and him alone shall you serve*." / then he led him to Jerusalem, made him stand on the parapet of the temple, and said to him, "If you are the Son of God, throw yourself down from here, for it is written: / *He will command his angels concerning you, to guard you, /* and: / *With their hands they will support you, / lest you dash your foot against a stone.*" / Jesus said to him in reply, "It also says, *You shall not put the Lord, your God, to the test.*" When the devil had finished every temptation, he departed from him for a time.

Brief Silence

For Reflection

By resisting the temptations, Jesus models for us how we are to respond to the inevitable temptations we face as human beings. In the desert he was faced with the balance between human need and divine goodness. He was mightily tempted, yet remained strong and never succumbed to the wiles of the devil. Twice the devil entices Jesus to give into temptation by saying, "If you are the Son of God . . ." Jesus resists the devil's temptation to put aside his humanity and act like God, thus remaining true to himself and to why he came.

But Jesus' resisting the temptations has implications for us, too. By fully embracing his humanity Jesus lifts us up to be who we are in our relationship with God. Only from this relationship do we have the inner strength and conviction to make right choices in face of the temptations that are an inevitable part of being human. Jesus resisted the temptation to act divine, and in this remained true to his identity also as being fully human. When we resist temptation, we remain true to our identity—an identity as both humans who are tempted and persons who share in God's divine Life.

♦ Some ways I serve others and strengthen those enduring temptations are . . .

Brief Silence

Prayer

Compassionate God, you love those who resist temptations and remain in communion with you. Help us to draw closer to you during this Lent, that we might celebrate Easter with the joy of those who know you intimately. We ask this through Christ our Lord. **Amen**.

Peter, John, and James went up the mountain with Jesus and saw his glory. Let us repent of our sins which mar God's glory in us . . .

Prayer

God of majesty and glory, your divine Son was transfigured and "became dazzling white." On our own journey to the cross, help us to encounter Jesus in his glory and be strengthened to do your will, embrace the cross, and one day share in the fullness of that glory. We ask this through Christ our Lord. **Amen**.

Gospel (Luke 9:28b-36)

Jesus took Peter, John, and James and went up the mountain to pray. While he was praying his face changed in appearance and his clothing became dazzling white. And behold, two men were conversing with him, Moses and Elijah, who appeared in glory and spoke of his exodus that he was going to accomplish in Jerusalem. Peter and his companions had been overcome by sleep, but becoming fully awake, they saw his glory and the two men standing with him. As they were about to part from him, Peter said to Jesus, "Master, it is good that we are here; let us make three tents, one for you, one for Moses, and one for Elijah." But he did not know what he was saying. While he was still speaking, a cloud came and cast a shadow over them, and they became frightened when they entered the cloud. Then from the cloud came a voice that said, "This is my chosen Son; listen to him." After the voice had spoken, Jesus was found alone. They fell silent and did not at that time tell anyone what they had seen.

Brief Silence

For Reflection

Jesus "went up the mountain to pray." Like us, Jesus sought communion with his God and Father. During prayer Jesus' "face changed." This phrase is biblical language indicating that Jesus himself changed. When the transfiguration takes place, Jesus is already on the journey to Jerusalem. To come to the glory promised by the transfiguration, however, Jesus could not remain on the mountain, but had to continue his journey to Jerusalem and the Cross. Luke explicitly relates the glory of the transfiguration to the glory of the new life that Jesus shares after his resurrection. Luke is the only synoptic evangelist who gives us a hint about the conversation among Jesus, Moses, and Elijah—they talked about Jesus' "exodus," that is, his "passover" which would be "accomplished in Jerusalem." This glory has a cost. And it is no small cost. It is one's very life.

On the mountain of transfiguration the disciples witnessed the glory of Jesus' identity as the "chosen Son." During prayer we, too, encounter God in such a way that we are invited to change. We, too, are emboldened to follow our life journey and embrace the Cross. And we, too, will be glorified. Now and forever.

♦ My ministry becomes a moment of glory for others when I . . .

Brief Silence

Prayer

God of Life, you clothed your divine Son in your own glory. In our communion with him and each other, may we open ourselves to all the gifts you offer us and one day share in that everlasting gift of the glory of eternal life. We ask this through Christ our Lord. **Amen**.

During Lent we are called to repent and bear the good fruit of new life. Let us reflect on how we have failed to use opportunities this week to repent and bear fruit . . .

Prayer

O ever living and loving God, you give us all we need to grow in our love for you. Help us to be open to how you cultivate this life in us, to be faithful to its promise, and to bear fruit in all we do. We ask this through Christ our Lord. **Amen**.

Gospel (Luke 13:1-9)

Some people told Jesus about the Galileans whose blood Pilate had mingled with the blood of their sacrifices. Jesus said to them in reply, "Do you think that because these Galileans suffered in this way they were greater sinners than all other Galileans? By no means! But I tell you, if you do not repent, you will all perish as they did! Or those eighteen people who were killed when the tower at Siloam fell on them—do you think they were more guilty than everyone else who lived in Jerusalem? By no means! But I tell you, if you do not repent, you will all perish as they did!"

And he told them this parable: "There once was a person who had a fig tree planted in his orchard, and when he came in search of fruit on it but found none, he said to the gardener, 'For three years now I have come in search of fruit on this fig tree but have found none. So cut it down. Why should it exhaust the soil?' He said to him in reply, 'Sir, leave it for this year also, and I shall cultivate the ground around it and fertilize it; it may bear fruit in the future. If not you can cut it down.'"

Brief Silence

For Reflection

The owner of the fig tree only cares about whether the tree bears fruit—he has no regard for the tree and its life. The gardener, on the other hand, cares about the fig tree, sees the life still there, and wants to give it every chance ("I shall cultivate . . . and fertilize it") to produce. He understands that as long as there's life, there's potential to bear fruit. He understands that it's not only the fruit that is worthwhile, but the very life of the tree itself. As long as there's life, something more can come.

Repentance is ultimately about life and about choosing life. Sin is selfishness, weakened or broken relationships, disregard for the value of life and what good can come from life. What wastes away life within us and prevents us from bearing fruit is sin. Repentance, then, means choosing to nurture new life and all the fullness it can bring. While the stakes are high (repent or perish, bear fruit or be cut down), the parable offers this hope: that in our work of repentance God shows us patience ("leave it for this year"), assists us ("I shall cultivate . . . and fertilize"), and shows great compassion.

♦ As a member of the Body of Christ I "cultivate" and "fertilize" the life and faithfulness of others by . . .

Brief Silence

Prayer

Compassionate God, you nurture us in many ways so that we can grow in the life you give us. Help us to choose that life, to bear fruit for your kingdom, and one day to share in the fullness of life with you. We ask this through Christ our Lord. **Amen.**

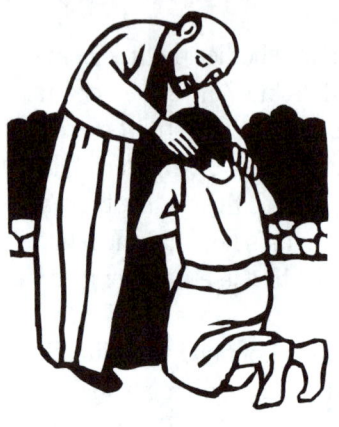

God invites us to the extravagance of the eucharistic feast. During our reflection and prayer, let us come home to God and ask for mercy so that we are prepared to come to the feast of God's love . . .

Prayer

Merciful and forgiving God, you welcome us back into your saving grace when we repent of our wanderings from you. Help us to choose life, to return home to you when we have strayed, and to open ourselves to your prodigal gift of Life. We ask this through Christ our Lord. **Amen**.

Gospel (Luke 15:1-3, 11-32)

Tax collectors and sinners were all drawing near to listen to Jesus, but the Pharisees and scribes began to complain, saying, "This man welcomes sinners and eats with them." So to them Jesus addressed this parable: "A man had two sons, and the younger son said to his father, 'Father give me the share of your estate that should come to me.' So the father divided the property between them. After a few days, the younger son collected all his belongings and set off to a distant country where he squandered his inheritance on a life of dissipation. When he had freely spent everything, a severe famine struck that country, and he found himself in dire need. So he hired himself out to one of the local citizens who sent him to his farm to tend the swine. And he longed to eat his fill of the pods on which the swine fed, but nobody gave him any. Coming to his senses he thought, 'How many of my father's hired workers have more than enough food to eat, but here am I, dying from hunger. I shall get up and go to my father and I shall say to him,

"Father, I have sinned against heaven and against you. I no longer deserve to be called your son; treat me as you would treat one of your hired workers.'" So he got up and went back to his father. While he was still a long way off, his father caught sight of him, and was filled with compassion. He ran to his son, embraced him and kissed him. His son said to him, 'Father, I have sinned against heaven and against you; I no longer deserve to be called your son.' But his father ordered his servants, 'Quickly bring the finest robe and put it on him; put a ring on his finger and sandals on his feet. Take the fattened calf and slaughter it. Then let us celebrate with a feast, because this son of mine was dead, and has come to life again; he was lost, and has been found.' Then the celebration began. Now the older son had been out in the field and, on his way back, as he neared the house, he heard the sound of music and dancing. He called one of the servants and asked what this might mean. The servant said to him, 'Your brother has returned and your father has slaughtered the fattened calf because he has him back safe and sound.' He became angry, and when he refused to enter the house, his father came out and pleaded with him. He said to his father in reply, 'Look, all these years I served you and not once did I disobey your orders; yet you never gave me even a young goat to feast on with my friends. But when your son returns who swallowed up your property with prostitutes, for him you slaughter the fattened calf.' He said to him, 'My son, you are here with me always; everything I have is yours. But now we must celebrate and rejoice, because your brother was dead and has come to life again; he was lost and has been found.'"

Brief Silence

For Reflection

This gospel parable is a familiar one and is often referred to as the parable of the prodigal son. On the one hand, the younger son is prodigal when he prodigiously squanders his inheritance. On the other hand, the real prodigality of the son lay in that he loved his life enough to swallow his pride, return home, and throw himself on the mercy of his father. While this son's situation was desperate enough—he was "dying of hunger"—he also knew his father well enough to know with confidence that he would not be turned away. He would not let him die. The younger son chooses life, even if it might be different.

The father, too, is prodigal: he welcomes him as son (not as a hired worker), clothes him in the finest array, and throws a lavish feast. The surprise of the parable is that the father expresses his forgiveness by restoring the younger son to their former relationship. He gave him new life. This is the most prodigal act possible: to give new life. The father chose life for both himself and his son when he restored the broken relationship.

♦ I love life so much that I . . . I have received new life from . . .

Brief Silence

Prayer

God of abundance, you prepare a feast for us who are faithful to you. May our communion with you constantly remind us that our only home is in you. We ask this through Christ our Lord. **Amen.**

Jesus does not condemn the adulterous woman, but he does command her to go and sin no more. As we begin our reflection and prayer, let us be truthful about our own sinfulness and ask for Jesus' forgiveness and mercy . . .

Prayer

Merciful God, we come before you knowing that we sin against you. Help us hear your word of forgiveness and resolve to return to you with all our hearts. We ask this through Christ our Lord. **Amen**.

Gospel (John 8:1-11)

Jesus went to the Mount of Olives. But early in the morning he arrived again in the temple area, and all the people started coming to him, and he sat down and taught them. Then the scribes and the Pharisees brought a woman who had been caught in adultery and made her stand in the middle. They said to him, "Teacher, this woman was caught in the very act of committing adultery. Now in the law, Moses commanded us to stone such women. So what do you say?" They said this to test him, so that they could have some charge to bring against him. Jesus bent down and began to write on the ground with his finger. But when they continued asking him, he straightened up and said to them, "Let the one among you who is without sin be the first to throw a stone at her." Again he bent down and wrote on the ground. And in response, they went away one by one, beginning with the elders. So he was left alone with the woman before him. Then Jesus straightened up and said to her, "Woman, where are they? Has no one condemned you?" She replied, "No one, sir." Then Jesus said, "Neither do I condemn you. Go, and from now on do not sin any more."

Brief Silence

For Reflection

The scribes and Pharisees bring an adulterous woman to Jesus and "made her stand in the middle." In their self-righteousness they wished to make an example of her as a grave sinner deserving death. Ironically, Jesus makes an example of them as sinners: they turned away from him and "went away one by one." Once they were faced with their own sinfulness and the futility of their "test," they chose not to remain with the One who would grant them forgiveness and mercy, reconciliation and new life. The woman, however, remained with Jesus. And for this choice she received forgiveness, mercy, new life.

Encountering Jesus always exposes the truth—both the woman *and* the crowd learn the truth about their own sinfulness. They and we are not all that different: we are all sinners who need to encounter Jesus, ask the truth about ourselves, and receive Jesus' mercy. Encounter with Jesus is the occasion for changing both the condemners and the condemned. Our own work during Lent is like that of the adulterous woman: truthfully face our sinfulness and faithfully remain with Jesus. Though we sin, Jesus only wishes new life for us.

♦ I remain with Jesus when . . . The new life I receive from him is . . .

Brief Silence

Prayer

O life-giving God, you judge us with truthfulness but compassion. Help us to turn from whatever takes us from you, open us to your presence of Life, and bring us one day to share in everlasting life with you. We ask this through Christ our Lord. **Amen.**

In the Garden of Gethsemane Jesus struggles to say yes to his Father's will. As we begin our reflection and prayer, let us examine when we have not been faithful to whatever God asks of us . . .

Prayer

O loving God, the love between you and your divine Son did not prevent him from embracing suffering and death. Help us to embrace dying to self for the sake of others and so increase our love for you by our loving others. We ask this through Christ our Lord. **Amen**.

Gospel (Luke 23:1-49 [Longer Form: Luke 22:14–23:56])

The elders of the people, chief priests and scribes, arose and brought Jesus before Pilate. They brought charges against him, saying, "We found this man misleading our people; he opposes the payment of taxes to Caesar and maintains that he is the Christ, a king." Pilate asked him, "Are you the king of the Jews?" He said to him in reply, "You say so." Pilate then addressed the chief priests and the crowds, "I find this man not guilty." But they were adamant and said, "He is inciting the people with his teaching throughout all Judea, from Galilee where he began even to here."

On hearing this Pilate asked if the man was a Galilean; and upon learning that he was under Herod's jurisdiction, he sent him to Herod who was in Jerusalem at that time. Herod was very glad to see Jesus; he had been wanting to see him for a long time, for he had heard about him and had been hoping to see him perform some sign. He questioned him at length, but he gave him no answer. The chief priests and scribes, meanwhile, stood by accusing him harshly. Herod and his soldiers treated him contemptuously and mocked him, and after clothing him in resplendent garb, he sent him back to Pilate. Herod and Pilate became friends that very day, even though they had been enemies formerly. Pilate then summoned the chief priests, the rulers, and the people and said to them, "You brought this man to me and accused him of inciting the people to revolt. I have conducted my investigation in your presence and have not found this man guilty of the charges you have brought against him, nor did Herod, for he sent him back to us. So no capital crime has been committed by him. Therefore I shall have him flogged and then release him."

But all together they shouted out, "Away with this man! Release Barabbas to us."—Now Barabbas had been imprisoned for a rebellion that had taken place in the city and for murder.—Again Pilate addressed them, still wishing to release Jesus, but they continued their shouting, "Crucify him! Crucify him!" Pilate addressed them a third time, "What evil has this man done? I found him guilty of no capital crime. Therefore I shall have him flogged and then release him." With loud shouts, however, they persisted in calling for his crucifixion, and their voices prevailed. The verdict of Pilate was that their demand should be granted. So he released the man who had been imprisoned for rebellion and murder, for whom they asked, and he handed Jesus over to them to deal with as they wished.

As they led him away they took hold of a certain Simon, a Cyrenian, who was coming in from the country; and after laying the cross on him, they made him carry it behind Jesus. A large crowd of people followed Jesus, including many women who mourned and lamented him. Jesus turned to them and said, "Daughters of Jerusalem, do not weep for me; weep instead for yourselves and for your children for indeed, the days are coming when people will say, 'Blessed are the barren, the wombs that never bore and the breasts that never nursed.' At that time people will say to the mountains, 'Fall upon us!' and to the hills, 'Cover us!' for if these things are done when the wood is green what will happen when it is dry?" Now two others, both criminals, were led away with him to be executed.

When they came to the place called the Skull, they crucified him and the criminals there, one on his right, the other on his left. Then Jesus said, "Father, forgive them, they know not what they do." They divided his garments by casting lots. The people stood by and watched; the rulers, meanwhile, sneered at him and said, "He saved others, let him save himself if he is the chosen one, the Christ of God." Even the soldiers jeered at him. As they approached to offer him wine they called out, "If you are King of the Jews, save yourself." Above him there was an inscription that read, "This is the King of the Jews."

Now one of the criminals hanging there reviled Jesus, saying, "Are you not the Christ? Save yourself and us." The other, however, rebuking him, said in reply, "Have you no fear of God, for you are subject to the same condemnation? And indeed, we have been condemned justly, for the sentence we received corresponds to our crimes, but this man has done nothing criminal." Then he said, "Jesus, remember me when you come into your kingdom." He replied to him, "Amen, I say to you, today you will be with me in Paradise."

It was now about noon and darkness came over the whole land until three in the afternoon because of an eclipse of the sun. Then the veil of the temple was torn down the middle. Jesus cried out in a loud voice, "Father, into your hands I commend my spirit"; and when he had said this he breathed his last.

Here all kneel and pause for a short time.

The centurion who witnessed what had happened glorified God and said, "This man was innocent beyond doubt." When all the people who had gathered for this spectacle saw what had happened, they returned home beating their breasts; but all his acquaintances stood at a distance, including the women who had followed him from Galilee and saw these events.

Brief Silence

For Reflection

Luke's Passion account highlights how much Jesus loved life. His struggle to say yes to his Father's will ("take this cup from me") was so intense that he sweat blood. He also intensely loved others and their lives: he healed the man with the severed ear, comforted the women of Jerusalem, forgave his executioners, promised Paradise to the repentant thief. For the sake of others' lives he was willing to give over his own life ("not my will but yours be done"). Already in his suffering and death Jesus is showing us that the very dying includes life-giving to others.

Jesus' concern for others in the midst of suffering speaks not only of his own startling self-giving, but also of the startling *value of the needy person*. Even when suffering Jesus loves the other so much! Jesus loves the life of the other as much as he loves his own life. Such is the care modeled by our Savior. Such is the life of his disciples. Jesus' struggle and self-giving is to be ours. While intensely loving the Life given to us, we also are to give it over for others.

♦ My manner of offering the Body (Blood) of Christ to others helps intensify their love of Life when . . .

Brief Silence

Prayer

God of power and might, you love intensely each and every person whom you have created. Help us to value others for their own dignity, embrace those in our midst who need our help, and open ourselves to the increase of love and Life you offer us. We ask this through Christ our Lord. **Amen**.

We remember Jesus' great love for us and his desire that we share this love with each other. Let us reflect and pray on this great mystery of Jesus' self-giving in the Eucharist by opening ourselves even more to God's love . . .

Prayer

Nourishing God, your Son gave us his Body and Blood as an everlasting memorial of his self-giving love. Help us to be servants like he was, to embrace humble service of others, and to love others with his overflowing love. We ask this through Christ our Lord. **Amen**.

Gospel (John 13:1-15)

Before the feast of Passover, Jesus knew that his hour had come to pass from this world to the Father. He loved his own in the world and he loved them to the end. The devil had already induced Judas, son of Simon the Iscariot, to hand him over. So, during supper, fully aware that the Father had put everything into his power and that he had come from God and was returning to God, he rose from supper and took off his outer garments. He took a towel and tied it around his waist. Then he poured water into a basin and began to wash the disciples' feet and dry them with the towel around his waist. He came to Simon Peter, who said to him, "Master, are you going to wash my feet?" Jesus answered and said to him, "What I am doing, you do not understand now, but you will understand later." Peter said to him, "You will never wash my feet." Jesus answered him, "Unless I wash you, you will have no inheritance with me." Simon Peter said to him, "Master, then not only my feet, but my hands and head as well." Jesus said to him, "Whoever has bathed has no need except to have his feet washed, for he is clean all over; so you are clean, but not all." For he knew who would betray him; for this reason, he said, "Not all of you are clean."

So when he had washed their feet and put his garments back on and reclined at table again, he said to them, "Do you realize what I have done for you? You call me 'teacher' and 'master,' and rightly so, for indeed I am. If I, therefore, the master and teacher, have washed your feet, you ought to wash one another's feet. I have given you a model to follow, so that as I have done for you, you should also do."

Brief Silence

For Reflection

On this night before he died, Jesus embarks on the most profound acts of self-giving fathomable. And he offers us the most unfathomable life: his own eternal life. Jesus offers others the fullness of life. We are invited to respond by choosing this life Jesus offers. This night Jesus showed the depths of his love for humanity: he gave us heavenly Food that promises new and eternal life. This night invites us: "as I have done for you, you should also do." We become truly alive and life-giving by partaking in the heavenly Food which transforms us more perfectly into being members of the Body of Christ.

Jesus also washed his disciples' feet. This self-giving act profoundly exemplifies for us how much Jesus loved life. It exemplifies for us how much Jesus wanted to give us life. It exemplifies for us what Eucharist truly is: self-giving, new relationships, new Life. We become truly alive and life-giving by becoming the slave to all by our own self-giving for the sake of others. We become truly alive and life-giving when we choose life by responding to others with dignity, reaching out to those in need, being for others the very presence of our loving God.

♦ Eucharist gives me life and helps me love more deeply because . . . I have chosen life when . . .

Brief Silence

Prayer

Gift-giving God, you give us a share in your divine Life as we eat the Body and drink the Blood of your beloved Son. Nourish us on our journey of life and lead us toward the fullness of life only you can give. We ask this through Christ our Lord. **Amen.**

Easter is the day for which we've been preparing during all of Lent; this is the day we celebrate Jesus' risen life. Let us pause to acknowledge God's gracious mercy to us and open ourselves to God's offer of new life . . .

Prayer

God of life, with great joy we celebrate the risen life of your divine Son. Draw us to the glory of this risen life, and never let us stray from you. We ask this through Christ our Lord. **Amen**.

Gospel (Luke 24:1-12)

At daybreak on the first day of the week the women who had come from Galilee with Jesus took the spices they had prepared and went to the tomb. They found the stone rolled away from the tomb; but when they entered, they did not find the body of the Lord Jesus. While they were puzzling over this, behold, two men in dazzling garments appeared to them. They were terrified and bowed their faces to the ground. They said to them, "Why do you seek the living one among the dead? He is not here, but he has been raised. Remember what he said to you while he was still in Galilee, that the Son of Man must be handed over to sinners and be crucified, and rise on the third day." And they remembered his words. Then they returned from the tomb and announced all these things to the eleven and to all the others. The women were Mary Magdalene, Joanna, and Mary the mother of James; the others who accompanied them also told this to the apostles, but their story seemed like nonsense and they did not believe them. But Peter got up and ran to the tomb, bent down, and saw the burial cloths alone; then he went home amazed at what had happened.

Brief Silence

For Reflection

Mary and the other women arose early in the morning to go to Jesus' tomb. This image of a new day speaks to us of a new beginning, new opportunities, new encounters. Early morning speaks to us of the freshness of new life. By contrast, Luke's gospel uses the word "tomb" seven times, speaking to us about the seeming finality of Jesus' death. By even greater contrast, this reading includes the Scripture certitude that Jesus "must . . . rise on the third day." Death is overcome. Death has no victory. God is the Lord of life. Easter celebrates a new beginning, our certitude of new life. May we choose that life.

This new life and dignity isn't something which can be measured or calculated or grasped. It is a freely given gift by the divine One who has loved us from the beginning of creation, who breathed life into us, and who continues to beckon us to grow into the fullness of life. In the morning we see the freshness of the dew fall, the glory of a risen sun, the clean smell of fresh beginnings, the sweet sounds of people waking to new beginnings, new certitude, new life. Easter beckons us to choose this life, this being with the risen One, this Alleluia that rings out our certitude in the God of love who gives us life.

♦ The "tombs" of my life are . . . What promises me new life is . . .

Brief Silence

Prayer

Glorious God of the living, you lift us from the tomb of our sinfulness and give us an abundance of life shared in Christ. Nourish us on our journey toward the fullness of life which we will one day share with you. We ask this through Christ our Lord. **Amen**.

We are a people baptized into Christ's death and resurrection. During our reflection and prayer may we be reminded of our baptism and of the presence of the risen Christ within us and among us . . .

Prayer

God of life, your Son's presence brings forgiveness and peace. Be with us as we struggle to live the risen life you have given us and to be faithful to your Son's command to forgive and heal. We ask this through Christ our Lord. **Amen**.

Gospel (John 20:19-31)

On the evening of that first day of the week, when the doors were locked, where the disciples were, for fear of the Jews, Jesus came and stood in their midst and said to them, "Peace be with you." When he had said this, he showed them his hands and his side. The disciples rejoiced when they saw the Lord. Jesus said to them again, "Peace be with you. As the Father has sent me, so I send you." And when he had said this, he breathed on them and said to them, "Receive the Holy Spirit. Whose sins you forgive are forgiven them, and whose sins you retain are retained."

Thomas, called Didymus, one of the Twelve, was not with them when Jesus came. So the other disciples said to him, "We have seen the Lord." But he said to them, "Unless I see the mark of the nails in his hands and put my finger into the nailmarks and put my hand into his side, I will not believe."

Now a week later his disciples were again inside and Thomas was with them. Jesus came, although the doors were locked, and stood in their midst and said, "Peace be with you." Then he said to Thomas, "Put your finger here and see my hands, and bring your hand and put it into my side, and do not be unbelieving, but believe." Thomas answered and said to him, "My Lord and my God!" Jesus said to him, "Have you come to believe because you have seen me? Blessed are those who have not seen and have believed."

Now Jesus did many other signs in the presence of his disciples that are not written in this book. But these are written that you may come to believe that Jesus is the Christ, the Son of God, and that through this belief you may have life in his name.

Brief Silence

For Reflection

What did the disciples *see* that brought them to rejoice? His wounds assured them that this was the Jesus they had seen die, the Jesus with whom they had walked the roads of Galilee, the Jesus with whom they had eaten, the Jesus who taught and encouraged them. His tangible presence in their midst assured them that the Jesus they see now is the familiar Jesus they know; he has come back from death to new life. Yet this Jesus is also different; his is a *risen* presence.

The disciples believed because they saw the Lord. We believe because we see the signs and wonders all around us of God's continued presence among us. We see and experience forgiveness, healing, peace, love exchanged, joy and laughter, beauty and growth, play and leisure, life lived to the fullest. Even now the risen Jesus continues to stand in the midst of the world through the signs and wonders worked by us who are his disciples. The risen Jesus gives his new life to us and sends us forth as his disciples. So what do others now *see* that brings them to rejoice? The risen presence of Christ in and through us.

♦ My ministry calls me beyond distributing the Body and Blood of Christ to living as the risen Christ in that . . .

Brief Silence

Prayer

God of peace, through our communion with you and each other we heal the wounds of strife. Help us to see all the gifts you give us, to grow in our love for you, and to cherish the new life you have given us. We ask this through Christ our Lord. **Amen.**

The risen Jesus revealed himself to his disciples and offered them an abundance of new life. During our prayer may God strengthen us to be a more visible witness of Christ's presence and gift of new life to us . . .

Prayer

God of glory, you do not look upon our weakness but call us to love and serve you. Be with us as we hear Jesus call us to fidelity and help us grow in the new life he offers us. We ask this through Christ our Lord. **Amen**.

Gospel (John 21:1-14 [Longer Form: John 21:1-19])

At that time, Jesus revealed himself again to his disciples at the Sea of Tiberias. He revealed himself in this way. Together were Simon Peter, Thomas called Didymus, Nathanael from Cana in Galilee, Zebedee's sons, and two others of his disciples. Simon Peter said to them, "I am going fishing." They said to him, "We also will come with you." So they went out and got into the boat, but that night they caught nothing. When it was already dawn, Jesus was standing on the shore; but the disciples did not realize that it was Jesus. Jesus said to them, "Children, have you caught anything to eat?" They answered him, "No." So he said to them, "Cast the net over the right side of the boat and you will find something." So they cast it, and were not able to pull it in because of the number of fish. So the disciple whom Jesus loved said to Peter, "It is the Lord." When Simon Peter heard that it was the Lord, he tucked in his garment, for he was lightly clad, and jumped into the sea. The other disciples came in the boat, for they were not far from shore, only about a hundred yards, dragging the net with the fish. When they climbed out on shore, they saw a charcoal fire with fish on it and bread. Jesus said to them, "Bring some of the fish you just caught." So Simon Peter went over and dragged the net ashore full of one hundred fifty-three large fish. Even though there were so many, the net was not torn. Jesus said to them, "Come, have breakfast." And none of the disciples dared to ask him, "Who are you?" because they realized it was the Lord. Jesus came over and took the bread and gave it to them, and in like manner the fish. This was now the third time Jesus was revealed to his disciples after being raised from the dead.

Brief Silence

For Reflection

The longer form of the gospel hints at two failures: the fishermen coming back with no fish, Peter's denial of Jesus before his death. Yet these failures became occasions for Jesus' gift of abundance: a large catch of fish, a fuller love that would "glorify God." Faithful discipleship is not measured by absence of failure, but by openness to obeying new commands from Jesus, recognition of God's abundant gifts, and willingness to grow into new life. While Jesus calls Peter (and us) to faithful love and discipleship, Jesus is also patient with us as we learn what it means to be his risen presence in the world, feeding and tending his beloved.

The questions, "Do you love me?" hint at faithful discipleship as a constant growing into a deeper love with the risen Lord. We don't express our love once, but constantly as we grow in our perception of the risen Lord's abiding presence to us and in our own ability to witness to that presence. As the gospel indicates, we sometimes will go where we "do not want to go." Peter's loving fidelity to the risen Lord in the end led to his death, the ultimate sign of his love for Jesus.

♦ The risen Jesus has manifested his love for me by . . . I manifest my love for him by . . .

Brief Silence

Prayer

Lord God, as you nourish us with the Bread of Life and Cup of Salvation, help us to nourish others by caring for them with generous love. We ask this through Christ our Lord. **Amen**.

Jesus is the Good Shepherd whose voice calls us to faithful discipleship. During our reflection and prayer may we hear more clearly the Good Shepherd's voice . . .

Prayer

O God, you speak words of love and comfort to us in the depths of our hearts. Help us always to say words to others that reflect your love and care and to seek out and be present to those in need. We ask this through Christ our Lord. **Amen.**

Gospel (John 10:27-30)

Jesus said: "My sheep hear my voice; I know them, and they follow me. I give them eternal life, and they shall never perish. No one can take them out of my hand. My Father, who has given them to me, is greater than all, and no one can take them out of the Father's hand. The Father and I are one."

Brief Silence

For Reflection

Our being "sheep" does not mean that we blindly follow Jesus, but that we actively pursue a relationship with him by hearing his voice and heeding his words. Although following the Good Shepherd truly leads to eternal life, the way of discipleship is not easy. But Jesus is both the Good Shepherd and the Lamb who was slain. As Shepherd, Jesus is the one who cares for us and leads us. As Lamb, Jesus is the one who lays down his life in sacrifice for us. However, nothing can interfere with Jesus' care for us: we are secure in his hands. We are never alone for he is the *good* Shepherd.

Hearing Jesus' voice and fidelity to its call involves us in the harsh realities of the world in which we live. Not everyone we meet wants to hear a message of forgiveness and repentance, of self-sacrifice and surrender, even when there is assurance that this is the only way to new life. Jealousy, violent abuse, persecution, expulsions, etc. have always been part of our human condition. No matter what challenges we encounter in following Jesus, nothing or no one can take us out of our Good Shepherd's hand.

♦ My ministry nurtures the security we have in Christ ("No one can take them out of the Father's hand") by . . .

Brief Silence

Prayer

O God who is Shepherd and Lover, never let us stray from your presence. Deepen our communion with you and each other and one day bring us to share everlasting life with you. We ask this through Christ our Lord. **Amen**.

Jesus gives us a new commandment to love others as he loves us. During our reflection and prayer, may God bathe us in the self-sacrificing love of Jesus . . .

Prayer

O good God, your love for us through the gift of the divine Son knows no bounds and lasts forever. Help us to love like Jesus did, with a willingness to die to self for the good of others. We ask this through Christ our Lord. **Amen**.

Gospel (John 13:31-33a, 34-35)

When Judas had left them, Jesus said, "Now is the Son of Man glorified, and God is glorified in him. If God is glorified in him, God will also glorify him in himself, and God will glorify him at once. My children, I will be with you only a little while longer. I give you a new commandment: love one another. As I have loved you, so you also should love one another. This is how all will know that you are my disciples, if you have love for one another."

Brief Silence

For Reflection

Jesus' new commandment is "As I have loved you, so you also should love one another." The nature of our love as disciples is specific, singular, incomparable: we are to love to the extent and in the manner Jesus loved. Our love is to be the self-sacrificing love of Jesus. It is this kind of love which brings Jesus glory. It is this kind of love which brings God glory. It is this kind of love which enables us to share in that same glory.

Yes, this love has a cost. This is a "new love" because it calls us to the same self-emptying as that of the slain Lamb. Our paschal transformation challenges us to make the norm of our love not self-love but the self-sacrificing love of Jesus. This is a demanding love because it will require that we die to self. Our dying to self brings new life, brings glory to God. This dying to self transforms the world! This love wipes away every tear and lasts forever. Our Easter joy is not found in avoiding its costs, but in embracing its price for the sake of the new heaven and earth it promises.

♦ My ministry nourishes and strengthens others to embrace the self-sacrificing love of Jesus in their daily living when I . . .

Brief Silence

Prayer

God our lover, you nourish us with your Son's own Body and Blood. May we cherish the Life that is given to us and spend it generously for others. May we love as your Son loved. We ask this through Christ our Lord. **Amen.**

During prayer we are privileged to rest in a special way in God's love and presence. Let us open ourselves to this God who chooses to be with us . . .

Prayer

O God who dwells within us through the Holy Spirit, you love us beyond compare. Be with us as we learn from your Son's words to us, teach us wisdom, and help us to love others more tenderly. We ask this through Christ our Lord. **Amen**.

Gospel (John 14:23-29)

Jesus said to his disciples: "Whoever loves me will keep my word, and my Father will love him, and we will come to him and make our dwelling with him. Whoever does not love me does not keep my words; yet the word you hear is not mine but that of the Father who sent me.

"I have told you this while I am with you. The Advocate, the Holy Spirit, whom the Father will send in my name, will teach you everything and remind you of all that I told you. Peace I leave with you; my peace I give to you. Not as the world gives do I give it to you. Do not let your hearts be troubled or afraid. You heard me tell you, 'I am going away and I will come back to you.' If you loved me, you would rejoice that I am going to the Father; for the Father is greater than I. And now I have told you this before it happens, so that when it happens you may believe."

Brief Silence

For Reflection

Jesus promises to send us the Holy Spirit who will "teach [us] everything." The Holy Spirit does not teach us *what* to believe, but to *believe*. To believe means to live out of the divine indwelling, live out of the peace given, live out of the mutual exchange of love between God and us and each other. Believing is living what the Spirit teaches us. Believing is an action that marries love with presence. God's love *is* divine life, divine indwelling. The Holy Spirit given to us *is* divine life, divine indwelling. The key to understanding the many parts of this gospel—loving, keeping Jesus' word, teaching and learning, receiving peace, believing—is divine indwelling.

Jesus' ascension paves the way for the Holy Spirit to come and dwell within us. This indwelling of divine Life teaches us to live with all the compassion and mercy, love and obedience, care and concern that exists within the Trinity itself. What the Holy Spirit teaches us is surrender of our very selves to God's Life within us, a surrender which prompts obedience to what God asks and opens us to receive the peace only God can give.

♦ When my believing in the real Presence includes believing the divine indwelling in others, my living looks like . . .

Brief Silence

Prayer

O God of life, you dwell within and among us and enable us to believe in your love and presence. Help us to live our belief, that we may be for others your love and presence. We ask this through Christ our Lord. **Amen**.

As we celebrate the risen Christ's return to glory at the right hand of God, we await the coming of the Spirit to clothe us with power from on high. Let us ask God to open us during our reflection and prayer to the power of the Holy Spirit within us . . .

Prayer

God of blessings, your Son blessed his disciples before he ascended into the heavens to take his place at your right hand. Help us to be faithful witnesses to his saving mission, to preach his Good News boldly, and to praise you always by the goodness of our lives. We ask this through Christ our Lord. **Amen**.

Gospel (Luke 24:46-53)

Jesus said to his disciples: "Thus it is written that the Christ would suffer and rise from the dead on the third day and that repentance, for the forgiveness of sins, would be preached in his name to all the nations, beginning from Jerusalem. You are witnesses of these things. And behold I am sending the promise of my Father upon you; but stay in the city until you are clothed with power from on high."

Then he led them out as far as Bethany, raised his hands, and blessed them. As he blessed them he parted from them and was taken up to heaven. They did him homage and then returned to Jerusalem with great joy, and they were continually in the temple praising God.

Brief Silence

For Reflection

Jesus' last earthly gesture toward the disciples was to *bless* them. In response, the disciples "did him homage" and experienced "great joy." This response was not to Jesus' departure from them, but was an expression of a new relationship to him, the risen One. Now, instead of *accompanying* him in his ministry, they were "clothed with power from on high" to *be* his presence and *do* his ministry. In essence, Jesus' last gesture toward the disciples was to *empower* them to be "witnesses of these things." His blessing empowered them to live a wholly new relationship with him, one that would be expressed in their obedience to his word, in their serving his saving mission, in their respecting his continued presence, and in their continued fidelity to everything Jesus had taught them.

Although Jesus "was taken up to heaven," the ascension does not end Jesus' work but inaugurates a new way of carrying it out: Jesus passes the mission on to his disciples ("you are witnesses of these things") and promises them the power to fulfill it ("clothed with power from on high"). The mission and the power are now theirs. With Jesus' ascension, the necessity of discipleship is clear.

♦ Where I have learned to depend on being "clothed with power from on high" is . . .

Brief Silence

Prayer

God of presence, your risen Son Jesus ascended into the heavens and commanded us to be his witnesses of the salvation offered to us. May we open ourselves to your Spirit's presence and be guided along the faithful journey we live that will lead us one day to share in your everlasting glory. We ask this through Christ our Lord. **Amen**.

Jesus prays that we be one as he and the Father are one. We ask God to bless us during our reflection and prayer and draw us into the unity that Jesus promises . . .

Prayer

O God, you are three in One and call us to share in your love and unity. Help us to witness faithfully to the unity we share as members in the Body of Christ and to lead others to the joy being one with you brings. We ask this through Christ our Lord. **Amen**.

Gospel (John 17:20-26)

Lifting up his eyes to heaven, Jesus prayed, saying: "Holy Father, I pray not only for them, but also for those who will believe in me through their word, so that they may all be one, as you, Father, are in me and I in you, that they also may be in us, that the world may believe that you sent me. And I have given them the glory you gave me, so that they may be one, as we are one, I in them and you in me, that they may be brought to perfection as one, that the world may know that you sent me, and that you loved them even as you loved me. Father, they are your gift to me. I wish that where I am they also may be with me, that they may see my glory that you gave me, because you loved me before the foundation of the world. Righteous Father, the world also does not know you, but I know you, and they know that you sent me. I made known to them your name and I will make it known, that the love with which you loved me may be in them and I in them."

Brief Silence

For Reflection

This Sunday's gospel—just a week before Pentecost—situates us with Jesus at the Supper with his disciples the night before he died. Jesus, always the loving one, naturally turns to prayer for his disciples: Jesus prays that the intimate love and union he shares with his Father may take root in his disciples. Experiencing such divine love and intimate union enables and sustains the disciples who are to take up Jesus' mission to the world. In fact, love and unity among believers is their primary mission, their first witness to the glory of the risen presence of Christ. Our love for each other is God's love in us spilling over. Our unity as the Body of Christ is God's life abounding in us in word and truth. This love and unity is a sign to the world about who Jesus is: the risen One united perfectly with his Father and with us.

This is the greatest compliment we can pay to Jesus: imitate him. Ultimately, this is what discipleship means: imitate him. This is how we are to live as disciples: imitate him. This is the call of the new life of resurrection: imitate him. This is the challenge of Pentecost: imitate him.

♦ Communion entails unity with the Lord *and* with each other. I foster communion with others by . . .

Brief Silence

Prayer

God of glory and love, you choose us to be one with you and call us to share that same oneness and love with others. Help us in our awesome mission to make your unity and love known, and bring us one day to share forever in intimate oneness with you. We ask this through Christ our Lord. **Amen.**

The Spirit of Love given at Pentecost is the Spirit present to us during our reflection and prayer. We ask God to bless and renew us in this Spirit . . .

Prayer

God of love, you imbue us with your graciousness and call us to share that love with others. As we celebrate the gift of the Holy Spirit, help us to grow in our love for you and each other. We ask this through Christ our Lord. **Amen**.

Gospel **(John 14:15-16, 23b-26)**

Jesus said to his disciples: "If you love me, you will keep my commandments. And I will ask the Father, and he will give you another Advocate to be with you always.

"Whoever loves me will keep my word, and my Father will love him, and we will come to him and make our dwelling with him. Those who do not love me do not keep my words; yet the word you hear is not mine but that of the Father who sent me.

"I have told you this while I am with you. The Advocate, the Holy Spirit whom the Father will send in my name, will teach you everything and remind you of all that I told you."

Brief Silence

For Reflection

"*If* you love me." "*Whoever* loves me." Our love is always a free choice and, as human beings, we are never quite sure of our choices. God's love, on the other hand, is sure and steady. God continually sends the Spirit to dwell within us. This indwelling Spirit empowers us to love with God's steadfastness. Transformed by the Spirit, our love moves from "if" to "I can, I choose, I will." On this festival of Pentecost which concludes our celebration of the resurrection, we are given a Gift of Life so that we can faithfully take up Jesus' saving mission. Pentecost is an invitation to choose to love, to choose to do, to choose to be risen Presence.

We can be sure of God's steadfast Love dwelling within us because God's very nature is to be love and God cannot act against the divine nature. God *is* love. The Father's love for disciples and Jesus' abiding presence with and in them *is* the Holy Spirit. Here is the import of Pentecost: divine indwelling ("make our dwelling"), outfitting for mission ("teach you everything and remind you of all that I told you"), and way of life ("love me . . . keep my commandments . . . keep my word").

♦ My distributing the Sacrament of Love enables communicants to know they are loved when . . .

Brief Silence

Prayer

O God, you nourish us with the Sacrament of Love. May the indwelling of the Holy Spirit increase our love for others and lead us one day to share everlasting life and love with you. We ask this through Christ our Lord. **Amen**.

In celebrating Trinity Sunday, we profess that our God is three divine Persons in One. This Trinity dwells within us. As we take time for prayer, let us reflect on whether we have appreciated enough this divine indwelling . . .

Prayer

O triune God, you are mystery revealed to us through the saving mission of your divine Son. As we are empowered by the Holy Spirit to continue Jesus' saving mission, may we never lose sight that you are always present to us and within us to help and guide us. We ask this through Christ our Lord. **Amen**.

Gospel (John 16:12-15)

Jesus said to his disciples: "I have much more to tell you, but you cannot bear it now. But when he comes, the Spirit of truth, he will guide you to all truth. He will not speak on his own, but he will speak what he hears, and will declare to you the things that are coming. He will glorify me, because he will take from what is mine and declare it to you. Everything that the Father has is mine; for this reason I told you that he will take from what is mine and declare it to you."

Brief Silence

For Reflection

The Spirit guides us to *all* truth. That truth is the Holy Spirit, is the Life given by the Spirit. *Everything* the Father has is given to us. What the Father gives us is divine Life. And it is for Jesus' glory that his disciples are empowered by the Spirit to bear what belongs to Jesus and the Father: divine Life. Our triune God holds back nothing from us. And here we have a double bold statement: our God is triune—three divine Persons in One God—and this God gives us everything we need to grow in the Life given to us.

The indwelling of the Spirit—divine Life—assures us of the *triune* God's working within and through us: the Father's love, the Son's mission, the Spirit's truth. We need not fear to take up the Son's mission; the gospel assures us we are not alone. Thus, the gospel illuminates two aspects of the Trinity. First, that every-thing the Father has belongs also to the Son and Spirit. Second, all that God has is given to us through Jesus who sends us the Spirit. Here is the great mystery and grace of the Trinity: the riches of God's own life are given to us, empowering us to take up the di-vine saving mission.

♦ Some ways I acknowledge, affirm, and build up the divine indwelling in members of the Body of Christ are . . .

Brief Silence

Prayer

Father, Son, Holy Spirit, you have given us all good things, even a share in your divine life. Nourish us and strengthen us so that we might be faithful to this life given to us. We ask this through Christ our Lord. **Amen**.

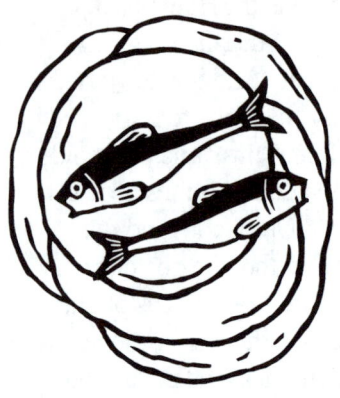

The Body and Blood of Christ sustains our Gospel call to self-giving. As we spend some time in prayer, let us reflect how we have faithfully given self for others . . .

Prayer

Generous God, you give us all good gifts, but especially the gift of your Son in the eucharistic Food and Drink we share. Help us to become more perfectly the Food that we share, so that our self-giving is our gift of praise and gratitude in return. We ask this through Christ our Lord. **Amen**.

Gospel **(Luke 9:11b-17)**

Jesus spoke to the crowds about the kingdom of God, and he healed those who needed to be cured. As the day was drawing to a close, the Twelve approached him and said, "Dismiss the crowd so that they can go to the surrounding villages and farms and find lodging and provisions; for we are in a deserted place here." He said to them, "Give them some food yourselves." They replied, "Five loaves and two fish are all we have, unless we ourselves go and buy food for all these people." Now the men there numbered about five thousand. Then he said to his disciples, "Have them sit down in groups of about fifty." They did so and made them all sit down. Then taking the five loaves and the two fish, and looking up to heaven, he said the blessing over them, broke them, and gave them to the disciples to set before the crowd. They all ate and were satisfied. And when the leftover fragments were picked up, they filled twelve wicker baskets.

Brief Silence

For Reflection

Healing, nourishment, satisfaction, and abundance are all signs of the presence of the kingdom of God. Jesus' actions in this gospel, however, reveal an even more telling sign. By taking, blessing, breaking, and giving the bread and fish, he foreshadows the total gift of his very self—on the Cross, in the Eucharist. The fullest presence of the kingdom of God is revealed by the total gift of self. When we receive Jesus' gift of self in the Eucharist and choose to be transformed into being that same gift for others, we are the visible presence of the kingdom of God. The kingdom of God comes to fulfillment in every act of total self-giving.

Jesus is the One who gave himself totally and continues to give himself to us in the Eucharist. In this Sunday's gospel Jesus not only fills the hungry with good things, he fills them to overflowing. This solemnity reminds us that Jesus' generous extravagance is not measured only by the amount of food but by the kind of Food he offers—his very self in his Body and Blood. The presence of the kingdom of God is an extravagant presence revealed in the signs of nourishment and abundance, in the signs of total gift of self.

♦ My ministry goes beyond formality to genuine self-giving—imitating Christ's own self-giving in the Eucharist—when I . . .

Brief Silence

Prayer

Bountiful God, you give us Bread from heaven to nourish and strengthen us on our journey of self-giving. Help us to open our eyes to the needs of others around us, to respond with your generosity, and one day to come to share forever with you at the heavenly banquet table. We ask this through Christ our Lord. **Amen.**

Just as Jesus gave life back to the only son of the widow of Nain, so does God offer us new life every day of our lives. Let us open ourselves to God's presence and offer of new life . . .

Prayer

God of the living, you have given us a most precious gift in the life we share. May we always be respectful of life, foster its quality in all others, and work diligently to share your life and love with others. We ask this through Christ our Lord. **Amen**.

Gospel (Luke 7:11-17)

Jesus journeyed to a city called Nain, and his disciples and a large crowd accompanied him. As he drew near to the gate of the city, a man who had died was being carried out, the only son of his mother, and she was a widow. A large crowd from the city was with her. When the Lord saw her, he was moved with pity for her and said to her, "Do not weep." He stepped forward and touched the coffin; at this the bearers halted, and he said, "Young man, I tell you, arise!" The dead man sat up and began to speak, and Jesus gave him to his mother. Fear seized them all, and they glorified God, exclaiming, "A great prophet has arisen in our midst," and "God has visited his people." This report about him spread through the whole of Judea and in all the surrounding region.

Brief Silence

For Reflection

The dead man was the widow's only son. Naturally, she was weeping. Jesus, out of pity, raised the dead son to life again, who "sat up and began to speak." He is alive! The gospel does not record the widow's response to this unexpected turn of events. It only tells us that "Jesus gave him to his mother." Perhaps her joy was too great to capture and record. Perhaps she was so stunned that she had no reaction at all. Perhaps she was completely taken up with the son's embrace, who might have been quite bewildered with the burial procession scene. But, really, how does one react to "He is alive!"

The crowd was in awe and "glorified God" for the miracle. Little did they know how in an even fuller and more life-giving way "God has visited his people." This God-man is an only Son, too. He, too, will die. He, too, will be raised up to new life. He, too, speaks. He, too, gives life. Then. And now, to us. When Jesus speaks to us the word of life—Arise!—he is offering us more than human life. He is offering us a share in his risen life.

♦ I see the glory of God on the faces of communicants when I . . .

Brief Silence

Prayer

Redeeming God, by raising your only Son to new life, you offer us a share in that same risen life. Help us to overcome anything that leaves us dead to you, grow in the life you give us, and one day share in the fullness of life with you in heaven. We ask this through Christ our Lord. **Amen.**

In this gospel a sinful woman touches Jesus as she washes his feet with her tears. Let us open ourselves during our reflection and prayer to this Jesus who will touch us . . .

Prayer

Forgiving God, your love looks beyond our weaknesses and embraces us even when we have sinned. Forgive us our trespasses and help us not to judge but be understanding and forgiving of others. We ask this through Christ our Lord. **Amen**.

Gospel (Luke 7:36-50 [Longer Form: Luke 7:36–8:3])

A Pharisee invited Jesus to dine with him, and he entered the Pharisee's house and reclined at table. Now there was a sinful woman in the city who learned that he was at table in the house of the Pharisee. Bringing an alabaster flask of ointment, she stood behind him at his feet weeping and began to bathe his feet with her tears. Then she wiped them with her hair, kissed them, and anointed them with the ointment. When the Pharisee who had invited him saw this he said to himself, "If this man were a prophet, he would know who and what sort of woman this is who is touching him, that she is a sinner." Jesus said to him in reply, "Simon, I have something to say to you." "Tell me, teacher," he said. "Two people were in debt to a certain creditor; one owed five hundred days' wages and the other owed fifty. Since they were unable to repay the debt, he forgave it for both. Which of them will love him more?" Simon said in reply, "The one, I suppose, whose larger debt was forgiven." He said to him, "You have judged rightly."

Then he turned to the woman and said to Simon, "Do you see this woman? When I entered your house, you did not give me water for my feet, but she has bathed them with her tears and wiped them with her hair. You did not give me a kiss, but she has not ceased kissing my feet since the time I entered. You did not anoint my head with oil, but she anointed my feet with ointment. So I tell you, her many sins have been forgiven because she has shown great love. But the one to whom little is forgiven, loves little." He said to her, "Your sins are forgiven." The others at table said to themselves, "Who is this who even forgives sins?" But he said to the woman, "Your faith has saved you; go in peace."

Brief Silence

For Reflection

The familiar and comfortable context of dining at table becomes an occasion charged with tension. The tensions are many: a sinful woman intimately touches Jesus in public, a host does not extend simple gestures of hospitality, others at table are indignant at Jesus assuming the power and authority to forgive sins. Simon and his guests not only judge the sinful woman, but they also judge Jesus. They fail to see who Jesus is: the One who came to bring the "good news of the kingdom of God." In this kingdom sinners touch God, receive forgiveness, and are granted peace. In this kingdom it is not tension and judgment that triumph, but love.

The issue is not whether we sin (we do and will!), but whether we will open ourselves to the judgment and mercy of God. This woman does; Simon, however, resists. Simon himself sits in judgment; the woman kneels in repentance. The gospel concludes with Simon being rebuked and the woman being forgiven. The woman's encounter with Jesus not only brought her forgiveness, but also was an occasion for her to show her "great love." Forgiveness is a sign of mutual acceptance, of peace sought, of love exchanged.

♦ My ministry witnesses to God's love and forgiveness abounding among the members of the Body of Christ when . . .

Brief Silence

Prayer

All-knowing God, you see into the hearts of each of us and forgive all that is not good and holy. Strengthen us by our communion with you and each other so that we can follow your Son's way of life more faithfully and one day share eternal life and holiness with you. We ask this through Christ our Lord. **Amen**.

Jesus in this gospel asks the disciples about who he is. As we take this time for reflection and prayer, let us open ourselves to encounter who Jesus is and choose to become more like him . . .

Prayer

God of the cross and resurrection, Peter revealed Jesus' identity as the Messiah, and then was faithful to Jesus' challenge to take up his cross. May we, like Peter, follow Jesus no matter what the cost and one day come to share in everlasting life with you. We ask this through Christ our Lord. **Amen**.

Gospel (Luke 9:18-24)

Once when Jesus was praying in solitude, and the disciples were with him, he asked them, "Who do the crowds say that I am?" They said in reply, "John the Baptist; others, Elijah; still others, 'One of the ancient prophets has arisen.'" Then he said to them, "But who do you say that I am?" Peter said in reply, "The Christ of God." He rebuked them and directed them not to tell this to anyone.

He said, "The Son of Man must suffer greatly and be rejected by the elders, the chief priests, and the scribes, and be killed and on the third day be raised."

Then he said to all, "If anyone wishes to come after me, he must deny himself and take up his cross daily and follow me. For whoever wishes to save his life will lose it, but whoever loses his life for my sake will save it."

Brief Silence

For Reflection

What the disciples answer as the general perception about who Jesus is—John, Elijah, a prophet—is in sharp contrast to Peter's confession of Jesus as "The Christ of God." What Peter doesn't know at this point, however, is that the Messiah is One who must suffer, be rejected, be killed, and be raised up. What Peter also doesn't know is that Jesus' revelation about his identity is a direct challenge to the identity of the disciples: to follow Jesus is to deny oneself and take up the cross daily. The dare of the gospel is that to answer who Jesus is, is to answer who his followers are.

It is an unheard of challenge to construct a self-identity in terms of denying oneself, taking up suffering and rejection that accompany faithfulness to the saving mission, and giving up one's life for the good of another and then to follow the One who promises these. But here is the point: to save our life, we must lose it. Yes, asking who Jesus is can be a very costly question. How do *we* answer who Jesus is? How do we live our answer?

♦ My daily cross looks like . . . For me, Jesus is . . .

Brief Silence

Prayer

Saving God, you help us carry whatever cross life brings us. Nourish us on our disciple journey; help us to be faithful and one day share in the fullness of life you offer us. We ask this through Christ our Lord. **Amen**.

Being Jesus' disciples means journeying with him to Jerusalem and the cross. Let us reflect on how faithful we have been in following him . . .

Prayer

Ever-faithful God, you never abandon us on our journey to Jerusalem and the cross. Help us to fear nothing along the way so long as we continually place ourselves in your care, knowing you are always with us to guide and protect us. We ask this through Christ our Lord. **Amen**.

Gospel (Luke 9:51-62)

When the days for Jesus' being taken up were fulfilled, he resolutely determined to journey to Jerusalem, and he sent messengers ahead of him. On the way they entered a Samaritan village to prepare for his reception there, but they would not welcome him because the destination of his journey was Jerusalem. When the disciples James and John saw this they asked, "Lord, do you want us to call down fire from heaven to consume them?" Jesus turned and rebuked them, and they journeyed to another village.

As they were proceeding on their journey someone said to him, "I will follow you wherever you go." Jesus answered him, "Foxes have dens and birds of the sky have nests, but the Son of Man has nowhere to rest his head."

And to another he said, "Follow me." But he replied, "Lord, let me go first and bury my father." But he answered him, "Let the dead bury their dead. But you, go and proclaim the kingdom of God." And another said, "I will follow you, Lord, but first let me say farewell to my family at home." To him Jesus said, "No one

who sets a hand to the plow and looks to what was left behind is fit
for the kingdom of God."

Brief Silence

For Reflection

As Jesus "resolutely determine[s] to journey to Jerusalem," he
encounters a number of conflicts. Jesus is not welcome in a Samaritan village, he rebukes disciples who want to take revenge,
he predicts the lack of comfort and security for his followers, he
chides those who have excuses for not immediately following him.
These conflicts arise because the journey to Jerusalem entails
death: dying to self in facing this journey's conflicts; death at this
journey's end. Nevertheless, the journey must be made—by Jesus,
by his disciples, by us—because this is the only journey that leads
to Life.

Single-mindedly following Jesus would seem like an ideal; yet
this is exactly what Jesus asks. We must put Jesus and his mission
ahead of everything—even more than the Law, even to the point
of putting into a different perspective our relationship to family.
We must put our hand to the plow and not look back. Is this possible? Not alone. But if we remember that as we follow Jesus to Jerusalem he is ahead of us leading the way, then it is possible—not
easy, but possible. We only need to say, "I will follow you wherever you go." And be absolutely determined to be faithful.

♦ The manner of my distributing Holy Communion reminds
others of the Life promised to those who faithfully embrace the
journey of discipleship when I . . .

Brief Silence

Prayer

God of life, your divine Son was persistent on the journey that
would fulfill his saving mission. Be with us as we travel his self-
giving path of love and help us one day to share the fullness of
life with you. We ask this through Christ our Lord. **Amen.**

Christ sends us out as laborers for his harvest. Let us reflect on and pray about how well we have labored and ask that we may rejoice now in the gifts God gives us . . .

Prayer

God of the harvest, your Son sends laborers into the fields of life to continue his saving mission. As we accept our own call to be good followers of Jesus, be with us as we bring Jesus' healing, peace, and life to all those we meet. We ask this through Christ our Lord. **Amen**.

Gospel (Luke 10:1-9 [Longer Form: Luke 10:1-12, 17-20])

At that time the Lord appointed seventy-two others whom he sent ahead of him in pairs to every town and place he intended to visit. He said to them, "The harvest is abundant but the laborers are few; so ask the master of the harvest to send out laborers for his harvest. Go on your way; behold, I am sending you like lambs among wolves. Carry no money bag, no sack, no sandals; and greet no one along the way. Into whatever house you enter, first say, 'Peace to this household.' If a peaceful person lives there, your peace will rest on him; but if not, it will return to you. Stay in the same house and eat and drink what is offered to you, for the laborer deserves his payment. Do not move about from one house to another. Whatever town you enter and they welcome you, eat what is set before you, cure the sick in it and say to them, 'The kingdom of God is at hand for you.'"

Brief Silence

For Reflection

Jesus sends the disciples out to plant the seed of the Good News and harvest its fruit of peace and the in-breaking of the kingdom of God. The "kingdom of God is at hand" because wherever disciples are present and received, God is present and received. Despite the disciples facing "wolves" and sometimes being rejected, their labor will bear fruit, for it is God's power that works through them. It is God's work.

Jesus admonishes the disciples not to keep their sights on the things they've accomplished, but on a future glory which still awaits them. The harvest is not what they did in accomplishing healing and casting out demons. The harvest Jesus sends his disciples out to bring in is the larger, even more abundant harvest of heaven. This labor is never ours alone. Without the power given to us by Jesus—the indwelling of the Holy Spirit—we would not labor fruitfully. For this divine power and presence, the disciples—and we—rejoice. When we are faithful to our discipleship, we share in the peace we offer those we meet.

♦ I bring the kingdom of God to . . . when . . . Its fruit is . . .

Brief Silence

Prayer

God of peace and love, your kingdom is present when faithful disciples proclaim the Good News and live what they proclaim. Help us to be good laborers for your harvest of salvation and bring us one day to enjoy the great harvest of fullness of life with you forever. We ask this through Christ our Lord. **Amen**.

In this gospel Jesus tells the parable of the Good Samaritan, instructing us to treat our neighbor with love and mercy. Let us open ourselves to the love and mercy Jesus offers us during our reflection and prayer . . .

Prayer

Loving God, you protect us, heal us, care for us. Open our eyes to the persons around us in need and help us to be Good Samaritans to all we meet. We ask this through Christ our Lord. **Amen**.

Gospel (Luke 10:25-37)

There was a scholar of the law who stood up to test Jesus and said, "Teacher, what must I do to inherit eternal life?" Jesus said to him, "What is written in the law? How do you read it?" He said in reply, *"You shall love the Lord, your God, with all your heart, with all your being, with all your strength, and with all your mind, and your neighbor as yourself."* He replied to him, "You have answered correctly; do this and you will live."

But because he wished to justify himself, he said to Jesus, "And who is my neighbor?" Jesus replied, "A man fell victim to robbers as he went down from Jerusalem to Jericho. They stripped and beat him and went off leaving him half-dead. A priest happened to be going down that road, but when he saw him, he passed by on the opposite side. Likewise a Levite came to the place, and when he saw him, he passed by on the opposite side. But a Samaritan traveler who came upon him was moved with compassion at the sight. He approached the victim, poured oil and wine over his wounds and bandaged them. Then he lifted him up on his own animal, took him to an inn, and cared for him.

The next day he took out two silver coins and gave them to the innkeeper with the instruction, 'Take care of him. If you spend more than what I have given you, I shall repay you on my way back.' Which of these three, in your opinion, was neighbor to the robbers' victim?" He answered, "The one who treated him with mercy." Jesus said to him, "Go and do likewise."

Brief Silence

For Reflection

"What is written in the law?" Jesus asks the "scholar of the law" in this Sunday's gospel. Many would tend to answer by citing the Ten Commandments or civil law. But the lawyer in the gospel answered correctly when he named love as *the* law. Law is not about keeping rules, or even organizing ourselves, but about loving others. And, above all, love is about relationships. Eternal life is not inherited by keeping laws, but by caring for others and treating them with mercy. The law of love teaches us to "love . . . with all . . . with all . . . with all . . . " Love is nothing less than the unconditional gift of self.

The parable about the Good Samaritan is a perfect example of unconditional gift of self. The Samaritan traveler "was moved with compassion" when he saw the half-dead man along the side of the road. But this kind man went beyond the minimum acts of bandaging the victim's wounds and taking him to an inn to heal. The Samaritan traveler left money for his continued care. Every detail about the Good Samaritan's actions models for us love as nothing less than the unconditional, ongoing gift of self to another.

♦ I see those coming for Holy Communion as neighbors to whom I must reach out with care and love by . . .

Brief Silence

Prayer

O God, your son Jesus modeled for us perfect, unconditional gift of self. May we be so inspired by his life that we care for others with his unselfishness and come to share eternal love with him forever. We ask this through Christ our Lord. **Amen**.

In the gospel story of Martha and Mary, Martha is more concerned about serving than about being present to Jesus. Let us open ourselves to Jesus' presence during our reflection and prayer . . .

Prayer

O God who is present to us, you call us to listen to you, encounter you, and serve you in others. Help us not to be anxious about many things, but to keep focused on you as the center of our lives. We ask this through Christ our Lord. **Amen**.

Gospel (Luke 10:38-42)

Jesus entered a village where a woman whose name was Martha welcomed him. She had a sister named Mary who sat beside the Lord at his feet listening to him speak. Martha, burdened with much serving, came to him and said, "Lord, do you not care that my sister has left me by myself to do the serving? Tell her to help me." The Lord said to her in reply, "Martha, Martha, you are anxious and worried about many things. There is need of only one thing. Mary has chosen the better part and it will not be taken from her."

Brief Silence

For Reflection

The gospel demonstrates many expressions of hospitality: welcoming, listening, serving. While each expression is valuable, none is complete in itself nor an end in itself. There is no one way to be hospitable. Hospitality in its deepest meaning makes possible a personal encounter of the kind that Mary is having with Jesus. This is the "better part" to which Jesus refers. Martha's generous hospitality is marred by her upbraiding Jesus and complaining to him about Mary. Rather than being truly hospitable, she is "anxious and worried" only about accomplishing a task. Her welcome shifts away from Jesus to herself. Busy about herself, she misses the "better part": centering on Jesus. The "better part" is to be undividedly present to the person of Jesus. Even when serving.

Hospitality—genuine welcome of the other and surrender to the other—facilitates encounter; one critical aspect of discipleship is being attentive to Jesus' presence. As important as certain aspects of hospitality are, the "better part" is to surrender to the presence of the Lord. Faithful discipleship depends upon keeping the Lord at the center of all we are and do. Faithful discipleship depends upon encountering the Lord.

♦ The sort of hospitality necessary in my heart in order to hear the Word and distribute the Body of Christ is . . .

Brief Silence

Prayer

Hospitable God, from the beginning of creation you welcomed us into your divine embrace by being present to us. In our communion with you and each other help us to live this hospitality and one day to share forever with you the fullness of life. We ask this through Christ our Lord. **Amen.**

In this gospel Jesus teaches the disciples the Lord's Prayer. Let us prepare ourselves to pray as Jesus has taught us . . .

Prayer

Our Father, you have been faithful to us in all things and so we are confident that our prayers will be heard. Help us to discern what it is you want for us and by our acceptance of your gifts always give you praise and thanks. We ask this through Christ our Lord. **Amen**.

Gospel (Luke 11:1-13)

Jesus was praying in a certain place, and when he had finished, one of his disciples said to him, "Lord, teach us to pray just as John taught his disciples." He said to them, "When you pray, say: / Father, hallowed be your name, / your kingdom come. / Give us each day our daily bread / and forgive us our sins / for we ourselves forgive everyone in debt to us, / and do not subject us to the final test."

And he said to them, "Suppose one of you has a friend to whom he goes at midnight and says, 'Friend, lend me three loaves of bread, for a friend of mine has arrived at my house from a journey and I have nothing to offer him,' and he says in reply from within, 'Do not bother me; the door has already been locked and my children and I are already in bed. I cannot get up to give you anything.' I tell you, if he does not get up to give the visitor the loaves because of their friendship, he will get up to give him whatever he needs because of his persistence.

"And I tell you, ask and you will receive; seek and you will find; knock and the door will be opened to you. For everyone who asks, receives; and the one who seeks, finds; and to the one who knocks, the door will be opened. What father among you would hand his son a snake when he asks for a fish? Or hand him a scorpion when he asks for an egg? If you then, who are wicked, know how to give good gifts to your children, how much more will the Father in heaven give the Holy Spirit to those who ask him?"

Brief Silence

For Reflection

Prayer is not magic; we cannot expect to receive whatever we want from God just because we ask. If this were so, many of us would be praying to win the lottery with great fervor! No, praying to win the lottery won't make us rich. But praying for what we need and what is good for us opens us to God's presence, helps us gain God's perspective on our lives, challenges us to think broader than our immediate needs. Prayer always includes a discernment of *what God wants for us*, not simply what we want for ourselves.

In this gospel Jesus instills confidence in his disciples that they will receive from God that for which they pray. He teaches them (and us) to pray for daily needs: the food we need to live, the forgiveness we need to grow in our relationships, the protection we need to remain faithful. Because of what we have already received (our daily needs), we are certain that God will give even more to those who ask: the Holy Spirit, a share in the plenitude of God's very Life. Such a Gift! Why would we not ask?

♦ I am most aware that in my ministry I distribute the plenitude of God's Life when I . . .

Brief Silence

Prayer

Our Father, you give us the Bread of Life to nourish and strengthen us and as a promise of the fullness of Life to come. Help us to give ourselves as daily bread to those who need to encounter your Life and love, care and goodness, forgiveness and mercy. We ask this through Christ our Lord. **Amen**.

In this Sunday's gospel Jesus warns us how foolish it is to place our hopes in earthly possessions. Let us prepare to receive the riches God gives us during our reflection and prayer . . .

Prayer

O God, you are generous to us in all things and give us more than we could ask or hope for. Help us to focus only on what matters to you and use the good things of this earth rightly for your honor and glory. We ask this through Christ our Lord. **Amen**.

Gospel (Luke 12:13-21)

Someone in the crowd said to Jesus, "Teacher, tell my brother to share the inheritance with me." He replied to him, "Friend, who appointed me as your judge and arbitrator?" Then he said to the crowd, "Take care to guard against all greed, for though one may be rich, one's life does not consist of possessions."

Then he told them a parable. "There was a rich man whose land produced a bountiful harvest. He asked himself, 'What shall I do, for I do not have space to store my harvest?' And he said, 'This is what I shall do: I shall tear down my barns and build larger ones. There I shall store all my grain and other goods and I shall say to myself, "Now as for you, you have so many good things stored up for many years, rest, eat, drink, be merry!"' But God said to him, 'You fool, this night your life will be demanded of you; and the things you have prepared, to whom will they belong?' Thus will it be for all who store up treasure for themselves but are not rich in what matters to God."

Brief Silence

For Reflection

The gospel is going far beyond "you can't take it with you." It pointedly reminds us that wealth isn't everything. In this gospel Jesus challenges the crowd to "guard against all greed." The rich man in the parable judges he has stored up enough possessions to guarantee a good life without worries—so he thinks. Any reliance on wealth and possessions, however, is pure folly—both worldly possessions and this life are fleeting. What truly matters is the inheritance that only God can give: the fullness of eternal life. What "matters to God" is spending our life dispossessing ourselves of anything which hinders us from growing into the fullness of life.

It is no wonder that we tend to lose ourselves in possessions—this is so much easier than pursuing only what matters to God! When we make the effort, however, to reorganize our priorities and keep our sight on God, then we gain what the man in the gospel never achieved—absolute security in our future. This is a future which is not in barns filled with grain and other earthly goods; this is a future in God! This future is eternal life!

♦ In order to be "rich in what matters to God," I need to empty myself of . . . This kind of self-emptying makes me more like Christ in that . . .

Brief Silence

Prayer

Good and gracious God, you call us to the fullness of eternal life. May our communion with you and each other help us turn away from being distracted by our possessions and turn toward what matters to you. We ask this through Christ our Lord. **Amen**.

God promises "inexhaustible treasure in heaven" for servants who are vigilant and faithful. Let us be open to the inexhaustible Treasure God offers us during our reflection and prayer . . .

Prayer

God of justice and love, you sent your Son as inexhaustible treasure so that we might always be ready when you make your presence known to us. Help us to be faithful and vigilant for the many ways you come to us and to be ready to receive you with open hearts. We ask this through Christ our Lord. **Amen**.

Gospel (Luke 12:35-40 [Longer Form: Luke 12:32-48])

Jesus said to his disciples: "Gird your loins and light your lamps and be like servants who await their master's return from a wedding, ready to open immediately when he comes and knocks. Blessed are those servants whom the master finds vigilant on his arrival. Amen, I say to you, he will gird himself, have them recline at table, and proceed to wait on them. And should he come in the second or third watch and find them prepared in this way, blessed are those servants. Be sure of this: if the master of the house had known the hour when the thief was coming, he would not have let his house be broken into. You also must be prepared, for at an hour you do not expect, the Son of Man will come."

Brief Silence

For Reflection

What, really, does the Father give us? What is the treasure that is to claim our hearts? The "inexhaustible treasure in heaven" the Father gives us is the Son (the Master). Our hearts must lie with the Son, for *he* is our Treasure. Those servants who are formed by this Treasure abide by the Son's expectations and seek to carry them out. Faithful servants do as the Son would do—their actions follow their heart. When our hearts lie where our treasure is, it is not overly difficult to do what the Son would do.

Jesus admonishes his disciples to be vigilant for the "master's return," to be eager to learn and do the "master's will," and to be "faithful" though the master's coming is delayed. Though much is required of them, more will be given to them: "your Father is pleased to give you the kingdom." In the gospel, the kingdom we seek is not a place, but it is divine Presence. It is manifested when we followers of Jesus are faithful to our Master's will. God's kingdom is present when we are engaged in an activity of "doing God." That is, when our doing is God-like: when it is creating and loving, merciful and forgiving, faithful and prudent.

◆ I am most aware that I am distributing the "inexhaustible treasure in heaven" when I . . .

Brief Silence

Prayer

O God, you are our treasure and our all. You are pleased to come to us and make your home with us. Help us always to be in communion with you and each other, that one day we might share the fullness of life with you. We ask this through Christ our Lord. **Amen**.

THE ASSUMPTION OF THE BLESSED VIRGIN MARY

On this solemnity we honor Mary who was taken body and soul into heaven to share the divine glory of the One to whom she gave birth. Let us prepare to encounter her Son, the source of our salvation, during our reflection and prayer . . .

Prayer

Saving God, your Son took on human flesh and was carried in the temple-body of Mary his mother. May we carry Jesus in our own bodies and declare the greatness you have done for us. We ask this through Christ our Lord. **Amen**.

Gospel (Luke 1:39-56)

Mary set out and traveled to the hill country in haste to a town of Judah, where she entered the house of Zechariah and greeted Elizabeth. When Elizabeth heard Mary's greeting, the infant leaped in her womb, and Elizabeth, filled with the Holy Spirit, cried out in a loud voice and said, "Blessed are you among women, and blessed is the fruit of your womb. And how does this happen to me, that the mother of my Lord should come to me? For at the moment the sound of your greeting reached my ears, the infant in my womb leaped for joy. Blessed are you who believed that what was spoken to you by the Lord would be fulfilled."

And Mary said: / "My soul proclaims the greatness of the Lord; / my spirit rejoices in God my Savior / for he has looked upon his lowly servant. / From this day all generations will call me blessed: / the Almighty has done great things for me, / and holy is his Name. / He has mercy on those who fear him / in every generation. / He has shown the strength of his arm, / and has scattered the proud in their conceit. / He has cast down the mighty from their thrones, / and has lifted up the lowly. / He has filled the hungry with good things, / and the rich he has sent away empty. / He has come to the help of his servant Israel / for he has remembered his promise of mercy, / the promise he made to our fathers, / to Abraham and his children forever."

Mary remained with her about three months and then returned to her home.

Brief Silence

For Reflection

In the song known as the *Magnificat* Mary is honest about who she is. Her honesty derives from her keen awareness of God's gifts to her. In response to Elizabeth's greeting, Mary not only proclaims the greatness of God, but also acknowledges that God "has done great things" for her. God's greatness and Mary's greatness commingle through her yes to being the mother of our Savior. God's greatness fills us when we, like Mary, say yes to God's plan of salvation and give birth to the Son through the way we live each day. The most honest we can be with and about ourselves is, like Mary, to acknowledge the great things God has done for us.

It is fitting that we thus honor Mary because it was her body which was the first temple for the Son of God. She conceived, nurtured, allowed to grow, and gave birth to Jesus—all because she willingly gave her body as an instrument for God to work the wonders of salvation. This holy body now enjoys full union with her divine Son in eternal glory. By her assumption into glory, God has "shown the strength of his arm" and the greatness of his love. God will do the same for us.

♦ I imitate Mary and proclaim the "greatness of the Lord" when I . . .

Brief Silence

Prayer

Loving and life-giving God, you did great things for Mary who chose always to be faithful to your will. May our communion with you and each other strengthen us to make good choices, to say yes to your will for our own lives, and one day to share the fullness of life with you and our Mother in heaven. We ask this through Christ our Lord. **Amen.**

Jesus was always faithful to his mission even to the point of death. During our quiet time with the Lord, let us pray that we may be strengthened to be faithful to him in all things . . .

Prayer

God of peace, you are the divine Judge who decides wisely and justly. Help us to overcome strife and divisions and sow the seeds of your love and faithfulness. We ask this through Christ our Lord. **Amen**.

Gospel (Luke 12:49-53)

Jesus said to his disciples: "I have come to set the earth on fire, and how I wish it were already blazing! There is a baptism with which I must be baptized, and how great is my anguish until it is accomplished! Do you think that I have come to establish peace on the earth? No, I tell you, but rather division. From now on a household of five will be divided, three against two and two against three; a father will be divided against his son and a son against his father, a mother against her daughter and a daughter against her mother, a mother-in-law against her daughter-in-law and a daughter-in-law against her mother-in-law."

Brief Silence

For Reflection

In this gospel fire is an image referring to divine judgment. Jesus is clearly stating that he has come to judge the people. His own faithfulness to this task and to his saving mission led to his great anguish and ultimately to his passion and death. So will we his faithful disciples be treated. Jesus' intent here is not primarily to condemn people, but to challenge them to right living according to the covenant established with God. So must this be our intent. Integrity of mission and commitment means facing opposition. The critical question for Jesus' disciples is whether or not we are enough on fire to continue his saving mission, no matter what the cost.

The pivotal point is that neither Jesus nor we *choose* division and strife; we choose to speak God's word and preach the values consistent with God's reign. Divisions occur simply by being faithful to God's message. This is the real shock value of the gospel: being a faithful disciple of Jesus will often instigate a clash of values, of principles, of priorities. The judgment we ourselves must make each day—and many times each day—is whether or not we are faithful to the Gospel values and challenges Jesus has taught us.

♦ The Eucharist brings me peace by . . . The Eucharist challenges me by . . .

Brief Silence

Prayer

God of justice and love, you are patient with our divisions and strife. By our communion with you and each other help us to heal our alienation from you and each other and to be faithful to the Gospel values Jesus teaches us by his word and life. We ask this through Christ our Lord. **Amen**.

In the gospel for this Sunday Jesus encourages us to strive to enter the narrow gate to salvation. Let us open ourselves to receive the strength God gives us during our time of reflection and prayer . . .

Prayer

O saving God, even though the gate to salvation seems narrow and the way difficult, you are always with us to strengthen us and beckon us on. Help us to give ourselves in loving service to others and keep us close to your divine Son at all times. We ask this through Christ our Lord. **Amen**.

Gospel (Luke 13:22-30)

Jesus passed through towns and villages, teaching as he went and making his way to Jerusalem. Someone asked him, "Lord, will only a few people be saved?" He answered them, "Strive to enter through the narrow gate, for many, I tell you, will attempt to enter but will not be strong enough. After the master of the house has arisen and locked the door, then will you stand outside knocking and saying, 'Lord, open the door for us.' He will say to you in reply, 'I do not know where you are from.' And you will say, 'We ate and drank in your company and you taught in our streets.' Then he will say to you, 'I do not know where you are from. Depart from me, all you evildoers!' And there will be wailing and grinding of teeth when you see Abraham, Isaac, and Jacob and all the prophets in the kingdom of God and you yourselves cast out. And people will come from the east and the west and from the north and the south and will recline at table in the kingdom of God. For behold, some are last who will be first, and some are first who will be last."

Brief Silence

For Reflection

The image of a *narrow* gate suggests stricture, difficulty, squeezing by. Entering the narrow gate to salvation is not guaranteed by privilege or tradition (those who perceive themselves to be first), but guaranteed by openness to the in-breaking of the Messiah (those who perceive themselves to be last). The gate is narrow because the way is difficult—journeying with Jesus leads to Jerusalem and the cross. The strength needed to persist on this journey comes from reclining "at [his] table in the kingdom of God." It comes from eating and drinking the messianic Food with the Messiah.

What is required of us? We must walk with Jesus to Jerusalem! Like Jesus, we, too, will meet opposition; we, too, must die to ourselves in self-giving to others. But we are not alone; Jesus is with us to support us and give us strength. We need only to keep close to him. We need only to keep our eyes on him rather than count the cost. Then we, too, can "recline at table in the kingdom of God" with him. His table is the banquet of eternal life. This is why the demands of discipleship do not overwhelm us completely. Sure, it costs. Sure, there is dying. At the same time there is also the rising!

♦ Like the Eucharist, I help others be "strong enough" to enter the "narrow gate" whenever I . . .

Brief Silence

Prayer

Nourishing God, you give us your Son's Body and Blood to strengthen us on our journey of embracing whatever crosses come into our lives. May our communion with you and each other bring us comfort and peace so that one day we enjoy the fullness of Life as we recline at your heavenly banquet table. We ask this through Christ our Lord. **Amen**.

The divine Host invites us to his banquet of generosity and love. Let us prepare ourselves to be humble guests who rejoice that we are called to this Table . . .

Prayer

Gracious and hospitable God, you call us to your banquet of love. Help us not to worry about places of honor, positions of power, or who are the other guests. May we always seek unity among your beloved people. We ask this through Christ our Lord. **Amen**.

Gospel (Luke 14:1, 7-14)

On a sabbath Jesus went to dine at the home of one of the leading Pharisees, and the people there were observing him carefully.

He told a parable to those who had been invited, noticing how they were choosing the places of honor at the table. "When you are invited by someone to a wedding banquet, do not recline at table in the place of honor. A more distinguished guest than you may have been invited by him, and the host who invited both of you may approach you and say, 'Give your place to this man,' and then you would proceed with embarrassment to take the lowest place. Rather, when you are invited, go and take the lowest place so that when the host comes to you he may say, 'My friend, move up to a higher position.' Then you will enjoy the esteem of your companions at the table. For everyone who exalts himself will be humbled, but the one who humbles himself will be exalted." Then he said to the host who invited him, "When you hold a lunch or a dinner, do not invite your friends or your brothers or your relatives or your wealthy neighbors, in case they may invite you back and you have repayment. Rather, when you hold a banquet, invite the poor, the crippled, the lame, the blind; blessed indeed will you be because of their inability to repay you. For you will be repaid at the resurrection of the righteous."

Brief Silence

For Reflection

In this gospel Jesus challenges both guests and host at a dinner. He calls the guests to let go of seeking places of honor and to choose seats that lead to being called "to a higher position." He calls the host to invite as his guests those who have only themselves to give in return, for which he will be repaid at the "resurrection of the righteous." Ultimately this gospel is about relationships. Relationships among ourselves that build upon true humility and unrequited generosity deepen our relationship with the divine Host who desires our presence at the everlasting wedding Banquet where we will be the honored guests. Jesus in this gospel brings us to a longer vision—not to be concerned with our immediate honor or satisfaction, but to put first what has eternal value.

We come to God empty and open ourselves to God's filling us with what is lasting. It is God who exalts us, not our own choosing or actions. It is God who repays us with the most unimaginable gift of all—everlasting life. Humility helps us shift our limited vision and relationship to an enduring perspective which keeps our focus on God.

♦ My relationships include . . . They lead me to Jesus when . . .

Brief Silence

Prayer

Almighty God, you call us into your presence and love us no matter how we come. Be with us as we strive to keep our relationships with you and others in right balance and bring us one day to share in the abundance of your heavenly banquet forever. We ask this through Christ our Lord. **Amen.**

In this gospel Jesus challenges us to calculate the cost of discipleship. During our reflection and prayer, let us ask for the grace to be faithful disciples . . .

Prayer

Lord of life and death, your Son calls us to follow him although sometimes this involves renunciation. Help us not to focus on the cost but on the gift of Life given to faithful disciples. We ask this through Christ our Lord. **Amen**.

Gospel (Luke 14:25-33)

Great crowds were traveling with Jesus, and he turned and addressed them, "If anyone comes to me without hating his father and mother, wife and children, brothers and sisters, and even his own life, he cannot be my disciple. Whoever does not carry his own cross and come after me cannot be my disciple. Which of you wishing to construct a tower does not first sit down and calculate the cost to see if there is enough for its completion? Otherwise, after laying the foundation and finding himself unable to finish the work the onlookers should laugh at him and say, 'This one began to build but did not have the resources to finish.' Or what king marching into battle would not first sit down and decide whether with ten thousand troops he can successfully oppose another king advancing upon him with twenty thousand troops? But if not, while he is still far away, he will send a delegation to ask for peace terms. In the same way, anyone of you who does not renounce all his possessions cannot be my disciple."

Brief Silence

For Reflection

Discipleship requires both renunciation and calculation. Those who wish to follow Jesus must renounce everyone and everything that gets in the way of a single-minded response to Jesus' invitation to be his disciple. At the same time, disciples are not naively to follow Jesus. They must calculate and consent to the cost—the price is giving their all, even their own life. What the One who calls gives disciples in return, however, is beyond calculation—fullness of new Life.

Jesus is using pretty radical language about renunciation and calculation in order to give us a chance to consider carefully what we do when we say yes to discipleship. Like so many things about life, we might enter into following Jesus with great enthusiasm and energy. But the cost of discipleship might soon dampen our spirits and lead us to lose sight of the gift of new Life Jesus offers us. Being a disciple is not something we can undertake halfheartedly or frivolously. It is a decision to be pondered and weighed. The cost is steep; like Jesus, we give our lives over for the good of others. Are we willing to pay the price? Every day? Do we calculate carefully?

♦ The price I must keep paying to be a disciple of Jesus is . . .

Brief Silence

Prayer

God of salvation, you are always faithful and never depart from us. When our energy wanes and our resolve falters, help us to find new enthusiasm and energy for the saving mission of your Son in your presence and strength. We ask this through Christ our Lord. **Amen**.

God cares for each one of us and seeks us when we stray. Let us reflect on God's compassion and mercy and open ourselves to choose God's gift of new Life . . .

Prayer

Shepherd God, you seek the lost and hold them dear to you. May we reach out to others as you have sought us and offer them the mercy, compassion, and forgiveness that you give us. We ask this through Christ our Lord. **Amen**.

Gospel (Luke 15:1-10 [Longer Form: Luke 15:1-32])

Tax collectors and sinners were all drawing near to listen to Jesus, but the Pharisees and scribes began to complain, saying, "This man welcomes sinners and eats with them." So to them he addressed this parable. "What man among you having a hundred sheep and losing one of them would not leave the ninety-nine in the desert and go after the lost one until he finds it? And when he does find it, he sets it on his shoulders with great joy and, upon his arrival home, he calls together his friends and neighbors and says to them, 'Rejoice with me because I have found my lost sheep.' I tell you, in just the same way there will be more joy in heaven over one sinner who repents than over ninety-nine righteous people who have no need of repentance.

"Or what woman having ten coins and losing one would not light a lamp and sweep the house, searching carefully until she finds it? And when she does find it, she calls together her friends and neighbors and says to them, 'Rejoice with me because I have found the coin that I lost.' In just the same way, I tell you, there will be rejoicing among the angels of God over one sinner who repents."

Brief Silence

For Reflection

What the shepherd, the woman, and the father all have in common is having lost something dear to them. When they find what they have lost, they rejoice extravagantly. In the parable of the prodigal son, he is found because he chooses to return to his father's house: he chooses life. By contrast, the older son—in his anger, resentment, and jealousy—is truly the one who is lost because he refuses to rejoice in his father's mercy and goodness: he chooses death. The extravagant mercy and goodness of our divine Father urges us to choose life over death. The challenge of this gospel is to let go of being lost and choose to be found; it is to let go of death and choose life.

God's response to our being lost (choosing sinfulness) is always one of mercy, compassion, and forgiveness. God is always faithful in giving us all we need to choose life over death. Being a faithful disciple does not mean always doing the logical thing nor the most practical thing. Like God we, too, must be merciful and forgiving. If we find this difficult, we only need to remember God's utter fidelity and compassion toward us.

♦ The lost I must seek are . . . I rejoice and celebrate when . . .

Brief Silence

Prayer

Compassionate and merciful God, you reach out to us and embrace us with the Food of life. Guide us in right ways and help us journey faithfully toward fullness of life with you. We ask this through Christ our Lord. **Amen.**

This Sunday the gospel faces us with the choice to serve God or mammon. As we settle ourselves into time for reflection and prayer, let us open our hearts to God's presence and guidance . . .

Prayer

Almighty God, you created us with free will and guide us to make right choices. Help us not to serve self, but to focus on the good of others. Help us to know which God we serve. We ask this through Christ our Lord. **Amen**.

Gospel (Luke 16:10-13 [Longer Form: Luke 16:1-13])

Jesus said to his disciples, "The person who is trustworthy in very small matters is also trustworthy in great ones; and the person who is dishonest in very small matters is also dishonest in great ones. If, therefore, you are not trustworthy with dishonest wealth, who will trust you with true wealth? If you are not trustworthy with what belongs to another, who will give you what is yours? No servant can serve two masters. He will either hate one and love the other, or be devoted to one and despise the other. You cannot serve both God and mammon."

Brief Silence

For Reflection

The wily servant has concern only for his immediate future and uses underhanded means to assure that his needs are met. By serving himself, however, the wily servant ultimately limits his world of possibilities. By contrast, disciples are to serve in such a way that they open their future to unending possibilities. Faithful disciples first choose not themselves nor the things of this world, but to serve God and others. This choice leads to an eternal future ("eternal dwellings"). At the end the gospel implies an important question related to the kind of future we deserve: Which God do we serve? The answer to that question determines whether or not we share in everlasting life.

The context for this gospel, then, is final judgment; the end is near and so we do anything necessary with prudence and decisiveness in order to be saved. Jesus is emphasizing what we must do in order to secure our desired future. We "make friends" with the things of this world as a means to an end: the end must shape our present behavior, our daily choices.

♦ The Eucharist keeps me focused on "eternal dwellings" in that . . .

Brief Silence

Prayer

Everlasting God, you trust us with our greatest wealth: being disciples of your divine Son and continuing his saving, serving mission. Help us be faithful and guide us in the right path during this life so that we might one day enjoy everlasting life with you. We ask this through Christ our Lord. **Amen**.

This gospel is the parable of the rich man and Lazarus. As we take time for reflection and prayer, let us open ourselves to God's presence so that one day we might join Lazarus in everlasting life with God . . .

Prayer

Caring and compassionate God, in you there is no rich or poor, only those whom you love. As you faithfully help those in need, also help us see and respond to those in need who are in our midst. Help us bridge the chasm of uncaring and build a span of love. We ask this through Christ our Lord. **Amen**.

Gospel (Luke 16:19-31)

Jesus said to the Pharisees: "There was a rich man who dressed in purple garments and fine linen and dined sumptuously each day. And lying at his door was a poor man named Lazarus, covered with sores, who would gladly have eaten his fill of the scraps that fell from the rich man's table. Dogs even used to come and lick his sores. When the poor man died, he was carried away by angels to the bosom of Abraham. The rich man also died and was buried, and from the netherworld, where he was in torment, he raised his eyes and saw Abraham far off and Lazarus at his side. And he cried out, 'Father Abraham, have pity on me. Send Lazarus to dip the tip of his finger in water and cool my tongue for I am suffering torment in these flames.' Abraham replied, 'My child, remember that you received what was good during your lifetime while Lazarus likewise received what was bad; but now he is comforted here, whereas you are tormented. Moreover, between us and you a great chasm is established to prevent anyone from crossing who might wish to go from our side to yours or from your side to ours.' He said, 'Then I beg you, father, send him to my father's house, for I have five brothers, so that he may warn them, lest they too come to this place of torment.' But Abraham replied,

'They have Moses and the prophets. Let them listen to them.' He said, 'Oh no, father Abraham, but if someone from the dead goes to them, they will repent.' Then Abraham said, 'If they will not listen to Moses and the prophets, neither will they be persuaded if someone should rise from the dead.'"

Brief Silence

For Reflection

The rich man in the gospel can neither see nor hear: he does not see Lazarus in need at his door; he does not listen to Moses and the prophets who guide him in right ways. The rich man is not in "the netherworld, where he was in torment" simply because of the good he received during his lifetime, but because his self-contained, self-satisfied lifestyle was not faithful to the teaching and practice of the Mosaic covenant. This is the rich man's sinfulness: he was so wrapped up in himself and his riches that he failed to pay attention to just relationships among those who are bound together in covenant with God. We who live today have even a further revelation beyond Moses and the prophets: we are to hear and put into practice the truth of the Gospel affirmed by Jesus who rose from the dead. By so doing, we choose now on which side of the chasm we will be in the next life. The chasm which separated the rich man and Lazarus is a gulf of uncaring. This gospel is a call to us: now is the time to act; once we enter the next life, the chasm will remain forever.

♦ To avoid the complacency and uncaring of the rich man, I need to . . .

Brief Silence

Prayer

Dear God, you call us into communion with you and each other where there are no chasms that separate us. Be with us in our daily living so that we might hear your word teaching us about who is in need of our care and love. We ask this through Christ our Lord. **Amen.**

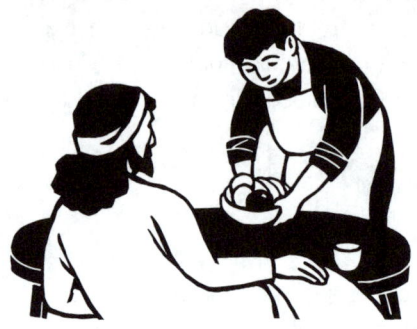

As we begin our reflection and prayer, let us open ourselves to God's presence and surrender to God's action within us so that our faith might be increased . . .

Prayer

Good and gracious God, you hear the prayer of those who cry out to you. Increase our faith, help us to do what you command, and bring us to a share in everlasting life. We ask this through Christ our Lord. **Amen**.

Gospel (Luke 17:5-10)

The apostles said to the Lord, "Increase our faith." The Lord replied, "If you have faith the size of a mustard seed, you would say to this mulberry tree, 'Be uprooted and planted in the sea,' and it would obey you.

"Who among you would say to your servant who has just come in from plowing or tending sheep in the field, 'Come here immediately and take your place at table'? Would he not rather say to him, 'Prepare something for me to eat. Put on your apron and wait on me while I eat and drink. You may eat and drink when I am finished'? Is he grateful to that servant because he did what was commanded? So should it be with you. When you have done all you have been commanded, say, 'We are unprofitable servants; we have done what we were obliged to do.'"

Brief Silence

For Reflection

Jesus tells the disciples that even a smidgen of faith can achieve great things. How do we increase faith? Faith increases through decisive obedience to what is commanded. How do we measure this kind of faith? We measure our faith by measuring our faithfulness. The faithful disciple of Jesus is never finished serving. The faith of a disciple is never finished increasing.

Faith is a way of life. Thus, the important thing to remember here is that faith is more a verb than a noun. Faith is expressed in the way we act. Faith is faithfulness. Here is the crunch: faith is truly extraordinary, not in the stupendous acts we might do for God and others, but in terms of the consistent and enduring choices we make daily to act righteously, humbly, mercifully, and justly as well as being forgiving and reconciling—that is, to be obedient to all that Jesus has asked of us. Faith is a way of living, a way of expressing our true selves such that we act toward others like the Divine has acted toward us. What increases our faith is faithfulness.

♦ When I witness my sisters and brothers in Christ receiving Holy Communion, my faith is increased because . . .

Brief Silence

Prayer

Faithful God, you are always present to us and your presence increases our faith. Help us to live the life you give us and to act in accord with your will all the days of our life. We ask this through Christ our Lord. **Amen.**

Just as the ten lepers in this Sunday's gospel ask for mercy, we begin our time of reflection and prayer by acknowledging our needs and asking God for mercy . . .

Prayer

Healing God, you care for those who seem alienated from relationships with others. May you touch us with your healing hand so that we might in turn touch others, healing all ills and strengthening the relationships among us. We ask this through Christ our Lord. **Amen**.

Gospel (Luke 17:11-19)

As Jesus continued his journey to Jerusalem, he traveled through Samaria and Galilee. As he was entering a village, ten lepers met him. They stood at a distance from him and raised their voices, saying, "Jesus, Master! Have pity on us!" And when he saw them, he said, "Go show yourselves to the priests." As they were going they were cleansed. And one of them, realizing he had been healed, returned, glorifying God in a loud voice; and he fell at the feet of Jesus and thanked him. He was a Samaritan. Jesus said in reply, "Ten were cleansed, were they not? Where are the other nine? Has none but this foreigner returned to give thanks to God?" Then he said to him, "Stand up and go; your faith has saved you."

Brief Silence

For Reflection

Sharing is fundamental to healthy relationships. In this gospel Jesus shares much with the ten lepers. They ask Jesus to take pity on them and he heals them. But only the Samaritan leper returns to Jesus, glorifies God, and gives thanks. This leper understands the give-and-take of healthy relationships. He reveals himself as someone who knew he needed healing, but also as someone compelled to return to his Healer, throw himself at his feet, and further the fledgling relationship begun with the healing. For this action he received even more than physical healing. He hears Jesus declare to him, "your faith has saved you." This is faith: knowing who we are before God, gratefully coming to God, and ever deepening our relationship with God. And for this we always give thanks.

The ten lepers exemplify aspects of our relationship with God: acknowledgment of need ("'Have pity on us!'"), obedience ("'Go . . .' As they were going"), and reception of divine mercy ("they were cleansed"). The Samaritan leper demonstrates another aspect of this relationship: only when he returns to glorify God and thank Jesus, does Jesus reveal that he has, in fact, been saved. For us, as for the Samaritan leper, salvation is revealed and experienced in the mutual sharing of an ever deepening relationship.

♦ What strengthens my relationship and brings me back to "the feet of Jesus" in gratitude is . . .

Brief Silence

Prayer

Gracious God, you give us so many good gifts that our hearts overflow with gratitude. Help us to increase the faith that saves us, and through our communion with you and each other come to share the fullness of life with you forever. We ask this through Christ our Lord. **Amen**.

In the gospel Jesus tells his disciples about the necessity to pray always. As we settle into our reflection and prayer, let us open our hearts to God's abiding presence . . .

Prayer

Lord God, you always answer our prayers and respond to our needs. Help us to be persistent in our prayer, to direct our prayer unselfishly for the good of others, and to increase our love for you. We ask this through Christ our Lord. **Amen**.

Gospel (Luke 18:1-8)

Jesus told his disciples a parable about the necessity for them to pray always without becoming weary. He said, "There was a judge in a certain town who neither feared God nor respected any human being. And a widow in that town used to come to him and say, 'Render a just decision for me against my adversary.' For a long time the judge was unwilling, but eventually he thought, 'While it is true that I neither fear God nor respect any human being, because this widow keeps bothering me I shall deliver a just decision for her lest she finally come and strike me.'" The Lord said, "Pay attention to what the dishonest judge says. Will not God then secure the rights of his chosen ones who call out to him day and night? Will he be slow to answer them? I tell you, he will see to it that justice is done for them speedily. But when the Son of Man comes, will he find faith on earth?"

Brief Silence

For Reflection

In this parable the widow's persistence in petitioning the judge is directed toward changing his mind so that he will act and render a just decision. Our own prayer is not a matter of changing God's mind, however. Persistent prayer is about faithful relationship to God that expands us and our expectations of how God is to act. God always acts justly. The challenge of the gospel is to keep on praying to a God who wills only good for us, who wills that we receive salvation and eternal life. Sometimes it is required that we must change *our* minds about that for which we pray or about our perception of how God answers our prayer.

Whether the response to our own prayer is delayed or speedily given, faith and hope uphold our efforts to "pray always." Persistence requires discipline, and it rests on the hope that the desired outcome of our efforts will be achieved. For example, we are persistent in exercise routines, athletic training, musical practice. So it is with prayer: we persist because of our hope that God will hear us, that our petition is just. This hope rests on the conviction of our steadfast relationship to the God who has always been faithful and who always listens to our prayer.

♦ For me to "pray always" means . . . What helps me persist through weariness and remain faithful in prayer is . . .

Brief Silence

Prayer

Just and merciful God, you never turn away those who turn to you in confident prayer. May our communion with you and each other teach us to pray for what is right and just and one day to be in eternal communion with you in heaven. We ask this through Christ our Lord. **Amen**.

Let us come before our God in humble prayer, acknowledge our sinfulness, and ask for God's mercy . . .

Prayer

O God, be merciful to me, a sinner. We trust in your mercy and love. Keep us humble before you and others, teach us the truth about ourselves, and help us to be justified before you and others. We ask this through Christ our Lord. **Amen**.

Gospel (Luke 18:9-14)

Jesus addressed this parable to those who were convinced of their own righteousness and despised everyone else. "Two people went up to the temple area to pray; one was a Pharisee and the other was a tax collector. The Pharisee took up his position and spoke this prayer to himself, 'O God, I thank you that I am not like the rest of humanity—greedy, dishonest, adulterous—or even like this tax collector. I fast twice a week, and I pay tithes on my whole income.' But the tax collector stood off at a distance and would not even raise his eyes to heaven but beat his breast and prayed, 'O God, be merciful to me a sinner.' I tell you, the latter went home justified, not the former; for whoever exalts himself will be humbled, and the one who humbles himself will be exalted."

Brief Silence

For Reflection

We've all heard the proverb "Too much of a good thing is bad," and this gospel surely points to this. The Pharisee is faithful to pious practices, even does more than he is asked. But Jesus does not praise him for his pious acts; in fact, Jesus renders the harsh judgment that he will not be justified. The Pharisee, for all his supposed goodness, misses the heart of prayer: inward turning to God that carries us outward to right relationship with others.

We cannot honestly pray to God if we judge harshly and set ourselves apart from those we meet every day. The tax collector is justified because he admits that he has not been in right relationships ("me a sinner"). True humility is honesty about who we are before both God and others. True prayer leads to God exalting us ("went home justified") because we have humbled ourselves before the Most High and have exalted others through our just actions toward them. True piety is directed toward humility and prayer. The issue here is not whether one ought to perform pious practices; of course we should! The real issue is whether those practices witness to our true selves before God.

♦ My spiritual practices and liturgical ministry lead me to humility and trust in God when . . .

Brief Silence

Prayer

Dear God, sometimes prayer is so difficult. Help us to be honest with ourselves so we can be honest with you. Teach us to trust in your mercy and forgiveness. And above all help us to know your love for us. We ask this through Christ our Lord. **Amen**.

This day we join the whole church in honoring all the saints who have gone before us, who live now, and those who are yet to come. During our reflection and prayer may we come to be stronger in our love for God and open ourselves to the holiness God offers us . . .

Prayer

Blessed are you, Lord God, for you are holy and you invite us to share in your life and holiness. Guide us along right ways so that we may never stray from the good example all the saints before us have given us. We ask this through Christ our Lord. **Amen.**

Gospel (Matt 5:1-12a)

When Jesus saw the crowds, he went up the mountain, and after he had sat down, his disciples came to him. He began to teach them, saying: / "Blessed are the poor in spirit, / for theirs is the Kingdom of heaven. / Blessed are they who mourn, / for they will be comforted. / Blessed are the meek, / for they will inherit the land. / Blessed are they who hunger and thirst for righteousness, / for they will be satisfied. / Blessed are the merciful, / for they will be shown mercy. / Blessed are the clean of heart, / for they will see God. / Blessed are the peacemakers, / for they will be called children of God. / Blessed are they who are persecuted for the sake of righteousness, / for theirs is the Kingdom of heaven. / Blessed are you when they insult you and persecute you and utter every kind of evil against you falsely because of me. Rejoice and be glad, for your reward will be great in heaven."

Brief Silence

For Reflection

What is our reward in heaven? The completion and fullness of
the kind of life we have chosen to live here on earth. Those who
choose the ways of God (poor in spirit, meekness, righteousness,
mercy, purity of heart, peace) receive—both now and in eternity—the reward of becoming like God. The blessedness of which
Jesus speaks is a quality of God—God's very holiness. The reward of the saints (those in heaven, and the faithful ones on earth)
is to be holy like God.

The saints we honor today are receiving their reward in
heaven. They are forever before the throne of God, giving God unending praise. Each liturgy, in fact, we join with all the heavenly
choir in giving God thanks and praise. Each time we celebrate
Mass we are united in a special way with all the praise offered
God in heaven and with all the saints who have been granted their
great reward in heaven. Thus, our celebrations now are a foretaste
of the glory—of the reward—which one day we will share with
these saints in heaven. Each of the Beatitudes in the gospel promises this same thing: those who are blessed now will share in eternal inheritance, the "kingdom of heaven."

♦ My favorite saint is . . . because . . .

Brief Silence

Prayer

All-holy God, you give us all we need to remain faithful to you and
to come to share the fullness of life with you and all the saints.
May we live the blessedness you bestow upon us and rejoice and
be glad for calling us to serve you in each other as did the saints
who came before us and whom we honor this day. We ask this
through Christ our Lord. **Amen.**

In our reflection and prayer this day we especially remember our faithful departed. We remember our loved ones as well as all those who have died in Christ. Let us ask God to help us to be faithful to the divine will in our own lives . . .

Prayer

Almighty and eternal God, you promise eternal life to those who are faithful. As we remember our beloved faithful departed, help us to imitate the good they did by always searching out and doing your will. We ask this through Christ our Lord. **Amen**.

Gospel (John 6:37-40 [see page 125 for other Gospel options])

Jesus said to the crowds: "Everything that the Father gives me will come to me, and I will not reject anyone who comes to me, because I came down from heaven not to do my own will but the will of the one who sent me. And this is the will of the one who sent me, that I should not lose anything of what he gave me, but that I should raise it on the last day. For this is the will of my Father, that everyone who sees the Son and believes in him may have eternal life, and I shall raise him up on the last day."

Brief Silence

For Reflection

We know physical death is the end of natural life; we Catholics (and many others) believe that there is life eternal. This is why we celebrate this feast day commemorating the faithful departed— we believe they live forever. We believe that God loves us so much that God wills we be united with the divine One for all eternity. The will of the Father is that Jesus not lose any one of his disciples nor "reject anyone who comes to" him. How comforting for us is this gospel teaching! The Father gives everyone to Jesus to form and teach and nurture into a gift Jesus can return to the Father. God promises salvation and eternal life to those who, like Jesus, do the will of the Father. The choice is ours to open ourselves to Jesus to be changed into a perfect gift for the Father.

Our remembering our beloved faithful departed on this feast day enables us to enter into the very mystery they now live: whatever happens to the faithful who have believed and died, will happen to us. Remembering, then, is a way to express our belief and hope. By uniting ourselves with the faithful departed, we embrace the mystery which we cannot understand: we embrace eternal life.

♦ As I consider my departed loved ones, my prayer is about . . . because . . .

Brief Silence

Prayer

God of the living, your divine Son desired that not one person be lost whom you gave him to bring to salvation. Instill in us the trust and hope that one day we will join our loved departed ones in everlasting happiness with you. We ask this through Christ our Lord. **Amen**.

Other gospel options for November 2:

Matthew 5:1-12a / Matthew 11:25-30 / Matthew 25:31-46 / Luke 7:11-17 / Luke 23:44-46, 50, 52-53; 24:1-6a / Luke 24:13-16, 28-35 / John 5:24-29 / John 6:51-58 / John 11:17-27 / John 11:32-45 / John 14:1-6

With great love God seeks us to save us. Let us prepare to encounter our gracious God during this time of reflection and prayer . . .

Prayer

O God of surprises, you do more than climb a sycamore tree in order to seek those of us who are lost. Forgive us our trespasses and help us to welcome your presence into all we do and say. We ask this through Christ our Lord. **Amen**.

Gospel (Luke 19:1-10)

At that time, Jesus came to Jericho and intended to pass through the town. Now a man there named Zacchaeus, who was a chief tax collector and also a wealthy man, was seeking to see who Jesus was; but he could not see him because of the crowd, for he was short in stature. So he ran ahead and climbed a sycamore tree in order to see Jesus, who was about to pass that way. When he reached the place, Jesus looked up and said, "Zacchaeus, come down quickly, for today I must stay at your house." And he came down quickly and received him with joy. When they all saw this, they began to grumble, saying, "He has gone to stay at the house of a sinner." But Zacchaeus stood there and said to the Lord, "Behold, half of my possessions, Lord, I shall give to the poor, and if I have extorted anything from anyone I shall repay it four times over." And Jesus said to him, "Today salvation has come to this house because this man too is a descendant of Abraham. For the Son of Man has come to seek and to save what was lost."

Brief Silence

For Reflection

Jesus did not intend to stop in Jericho, but Zacchaeus stopped him short! Jesus responds to Zacchaeus's uninhibited enthusiasm by doing for him the very thing Jesus came to do: "to seek out and to save what was lost." Their dramatic encounter brings out something about each of them which has escaped the grumbling crowd: Zacchaeus is open to being changed through an encounter with Jesus; Jesus is the One who inspires the kind of change that leads to salvation. We are to be just as uninhibited and enthusiastic about encountering Jesus and just as willing to be changed by him. When we truly encounter Jesus, the one who is compassionate toward those who seem lost, our lives can never be the same. Like Zacchaeus, we are changed.

Because of his encounter with Jesus, Zacchaeus receives Jesus into his own home "with joy." Moreover, this encounter brings a changed behavior in Zacchaeus: he shares his wealth with the poor and mends his sinful ways. Because of this, Jesus says to him, "Today salvation has come to this house." The dignity of means and status (Zacchaeus was a wealthy tax collector) is nothing compared to the dignity God bestows on forgiven sinners who are saved.

♦ As I distribute Holy Communion, I delight in the Son of Man coming "to seek and to save what was lost" when I . . .

Brief Silence

Prayer

God of justice and mercy, you forgive us our sins and offer us salvation. Help us to seek you diligently, to rejoice when we recognize your presence, and to invite you to abide within us. We ask this through Christ our Lord. **Amen**.

In the Creed we profess our belief in the resurrection from the dead and the gift of everlasting life. In this hope, let us spend our time in reflection and prayer before our loving God . . .

Prayer

God of the living, you sustain our life now and call us to a share in your everlasting life. Help us to respect all life and to see your creative hand in all the life that surrounds us. We ask this through Christ our Lord. **Amen**.

Gospel (Luke 20:27, 34-38 [Longer Form: Luke 20:27-38])

Some Sadducees, those who deny that there is a resurrection, came forward.

Jesus said to them, "The children of this age marry and re-marry; but those who are deemed worthy to attain to the coming age and to the resurrection of the dead neither marry nor are given in marriage. They can no longer die, for they are like angels; and they are the children of God because they are the ones who will rise. That the dead will rise even Moses made known in the passage about the bush, when he called out 'Lord,' the God of Abraham, the God of Isaac, and the God of Jacob; and he is not God of the dead, but of the living, for to him all are alive."

Brief Silence

For Reflection

As baptized Christians, we align ourselves with Jesus who teaches resurrection and eternal life shared with him in glory. Nonetheless, our belief in Jesus and the resurrection makes eternal life no less a mystery. We believe, however, because Jesus has died and risen. He has gone before us. He has shown us the way. His victory is our sure hope. Our choices today about whether we follow Jesus faithfully and live Gospel values by dying to ourselves for the good of others reveal the extent of our own hope in sharing in Jesus' risen life. In no uncertain terms, Jesus affirms resurrection and eternal life.

The Sadducees are fixated on dying; Jesus is focused on living. The Sadducees deny there is resurrection; Jesus proves there is by rising from the dead. The Sadducees are trapped by affairs of this life; Jesus abides with the angels and "the children of God . . . who will rise." The Sadducees' idea of this life ends with death: there is nothing more. Jesus knows that this life continues in newness of life. And there is even more: we already participate in what the Sadducees deny. To God "all are alive" *now*.

♦ I am drawn to reflect on rising from the dead and eternal life when . . .

Brief Silence

Prayer

God of the resurrection, our hope in eternal life lies in your raising your beloved Son from the dead. Help us to be faithful to the Gospel he taught us and one day share in the fullness of salvation, life everlasting with you. We ask this through Christ our Lord. **Amen**.

In the day of Christ's coming, wrong will be righted, suffering will end, death will yield to eternal life. Let us prepare to meet Christ who comes to us through our reflection and prayer . . .

Prayer

God of hope and promise, you are with us until the end of time. Ease our fears in face of the world catastrophes we experience and instill in us the confidence we need to be faithful in continuing Jesus' saving mission. We ask this through Christ our Lord. **Amen**.

Gospel (Luke 21:5-19)

While some people were speaking about how the temple was adorned with costly stones and votive offerings, Jesus said, "All that you see here—the days will come when there will not be left a stone upon another stone that will not be thrown down."

Then they asked him, "Teacher, when will this happen? And what sign will there be when all these things are about to happen?" He answered, "See that you not be deceived, for many will come in my name, saying, 'I am he,' and 'The time has come.' Do not follow them! When you hear of wars and insurrections, do not be terrified; for such things must happen first, but it will not immediately be the end." Then he said to them, "Nation will rise against nation, and kingdom against kingdom. There will be powerful earthquakes, famines, and plagues from place to place; and awesome sights and mighty signs will come from the sky.

"Before all this happens, however, they will seize and persecute you, they will hand you over to the synagogues and to prisons, and they will have you led before kings and governors because of my name. It will lead to your giving testimony. Remember, you are not to prepare your defense beforehand, for I myself shall give you a wisdom in speaking that all your adversaries will be powerless to resist or refute. You will even be handed over by parents, brothers, relatives, and friends, and they will put some of you to death. You will be hated by all because of my name, but not a hair on your head will be destroyed. By your perseverance you will secure your lives."

Brief Silence

For Reflection

The readings for this Sunday are really filled with hope, not doom or fear. Along with all these terrifying things, good things happen: Jesus assures us that he will be the victor ("all your adversaries will be powerless to resist or refute"). Catastrophes, disasters, wars, insurrections, etc., are not signs of the end of the world, but of how far we actually are from the end. We hasten the end not by being fearful of these events, but by being faithful to Jesus' work of establishing God's kingdom. Preaching, teaching, and living in Jesus' name is the one sure way of discipleship that hastens Jesus' Second Coming and secures for us eternal life. We will know the end is near not by increased terror and hardship, rampant evil and lack of care for each other, constant upset and loss. The end is near when goodness and love are abundant, when caring and sharing mark our daily living, when all people are brothers and sisters. The end is marked by goodness, not by evil. When God's reign of peace and justice is established throughout our world, the end will be here. There will be no more work of salvation to do.

♦ At Eucharist I celebrate my life secure in Christ because . . . I share this security with others by . . .

Brief Silence

Prayer

Gracious God of judgment and life, our communion with you and each other prepares us to receive the fullness of life you offer us. Help us to be faithful to Jesus' Gospel and may we experience joy in knowing that you invite us to hasten the establishment of your reign by the goodness of our lives. We ask this through Christ our Lord. **Amen.**

We come together to honor Christ our King. As we spend time in reflection and prayer, let us open ourselves to his call to share fullness of life with him in Paradise . . .

Prayer

O God who reigns over us with compassion and love, you desire that all of us share in the risen life of Christ our King. May we be faithful to the daily demands of Gospel living and generously give ourselves over for the good of others. We ask this through Christ our Lord. **Amen**.

Gospel (Luke 23:35-43)

The rulers sneered at Jesus and said, "He saved others, let him save himself if he is the chosen one, the Christ of God." Even the soldiers jeered at him. As they approached to offer him wine they called out, "If you are King of the Jews, save yourself." Above him there was an inscription that read, "This is the King of the Jews."

Now one of the criminals hanging there reviled Jesus, saying, "Are you not the Christ? Save yourself and us." The other, however, rebuking him, said in reply, "Have you no fear of God, for you are subject to the same condemnation? And indeed, we have been condemned justly, for the sentence we received corresponds to our crimes, but this man has done nothing criminal." Then he said, "Jesus, remember me when you come into your kingdom." He replied to him, "Amen, I say to you, today you will be with me in Paradise."

Brief Silence

For Reflection

"If you are King . . . save yourself" the soldiers jeered at Jesus on the cross. So did the rulers and one criminal crucified with Jesus taunt him about saving himself. But they misunderstand what "save yourself" means and what motivated Jesus to live the way he did. The rulers, soldiers, and one criminal thought being saved meant that Jesus should come down from the cross, avoid any more suffering, certainly avoid death. But Jesus shows us through his words to the other criminal what being saved really means: "you will be with me in Paradise." Salvation is less a matter of being saved *from*, than a matter of being saved *for*.

Like Jesus, we cannot save ourselves from the daily demands of faithful discipleship. We cannot avoid accepting our daily cross in living as he did, giving ourselves for the sake of others. The kingdom of God is among us, in us, and through us to the extent that we open ourselves to his risen Presence among us, in us, and through us. Being saved is a matter of embracing this Presence, living it, and allowing it to shape who we are, the decisions we make for daily living, and why we choose to follow our King through the cross to fullness of life.

♦ I distribute Christ the King at Eucharist; I "distribute" Christ's reign whenever . . .

Brief Silence

Prayer

O God, we freely place ourselves under your sovereign care. As we hail your divine Son as Christ, the King of the universe, open our hearts wide to accept all those who are seeking you with sincere hearts. Bring all of us into your everlasting kingdom. We ask this through Christ our Lord. **Amen.**